Bob
As Life Goes On: Lessons One Doesn't Want to Have to Learn

by

Rosalie H. Contino, PhD

Dear Laura,

1-2013

We never know what life has in store for us.

Rosalie H. Contino PhD

DORRANCE PUBLISHING CO., INC.
PITTSBURGH, PENNSYLVANIA 15222

Dorrance Publishing Co., Inc.
701 Smithfield Street
Pittsburgh, PA 15222
Visit our website at *www.dorrancebookstore.com*

ISBN: 978-1-4349-2840-5
eISBN: 978-1-4349-2192-5

The high school photo from Lafayette High School, June 1958

Bob

As Life Goes On: Lessons One Doesn't Want to Have to Learn

by

Rosalie H. Contino, PhD

A sister reflects on the life of her brother as she relates her experience as his caretaker.

Contents

Preface

You know, I had an eye operation for a double cross in my eye. I had to go back for another one, and I still had to wear glasses. I went into the hospital for tonsils and had to have the adenoid taken out. They also thought I had meningitis but it was a good thing I didn't. Maybe I wouldn't be here talking about it. I wore braces to straighten out my teeth and wound up with a lot of cavities. As result, I needed caps and they didn't last too long because they broke or cracked.

Even my head wasn't put on straight. What happened to me? Why did all these things happen only to me?

My mother and I both had a long cry when she told me the story about Bob's feelings about himself. It seemed, to put it into a nutshell, a life full of pain and frustration. We cried because we loved Bob. And we cried, I think, from our own sense of helplessness, our having to sit on the sidelines and help him pick up the pieces as best we could, being unable to prevent him from being afflicted in the first place. Like Bob, and like Job before him, we wondered why these evils or hardships visited on us.

People work hard trying to carve out a niche for themselves in society or in a career that we take the little incidentals of our life for granted. For many of us, through much of our lives, the day-to-day part of our existence is a given. We expect to be reasonably healthy, and we expect one day to pretty much follow another. Our energy is devoted to achieving success, whatever that means to us at the moment. Only when we have it shoved in our face do we realize that those little incidentals are really the most important things of all, and how fragile our boat of dreams really is.

My brother was always my brother and will always be my brother. And I never thought anything of it until Mom died on November 11, 1985. That is a day I will never forget, since it not only marked the passing of a great lady, but also marked my transformation into "Mrs. Mom" to Dad and my brother.

Mom herself recognized that I would have to assume her role in the family. Just before she died, she insisted, "Don't forget to keep an eye on your brother!" She held my hand and said again, "Don't forget!" I nodded "yes" since I could not get my voice past the lump in my throat. Little did I realize what that passing of responsibility would mean over the next twenty and more years.

Though reflecting on my family's experiences since Bob first became ill in 1963, maybe I *should* have known better what to expect. Then again, there is always the hope that life would just somehow, someway, get back to normal. And normal was *so* good!

Acknowledgments

I have to thank the following for their guidance, suggestions, and patience: Palma Arena, Nettie Arena, Katherine Baccaro, Cindy Beharry, Danny Clancy, Roberta Conway, Mary Jane Di Massi, Cathy Goldsmith, Eleanor Grillo, Charlotte Grosso, Rose Golub, Diane Orr, Rosalind Panepento, Belle Plavé, Luisa Plavé, Suzanne Plavé, Marie Pionegro, Salvatore Potestivo, Alba Savage and with Jodi and Alan Siegel, Dr. Edgar and Mary Lou Schweikert, Ann Marie Salerno, Gerri Troisi-Torres.

Thanks to Richard Hresko of QED Professional Preparation Services, LLC for his technical assistance in helping to ready this book for publication."

I thank the following doctors for their sense of commitment and professionalism in caring for my brother, Bob.

Dr. Paul Maravel, MD, Dr. Robert Miele, podiatrist, Dr. Bo Shim cardiologist.

For his ongoing guidance. Andrew Sichenze, attorney.

Dad, Bob and me at the Dyker Park Bklyn, NY

In the Beginning

We led very simple lives starting with our names. My mother made sure that our names were "American" with nice nicknames. She herself, the last of ten children, was called Domenica (Sunday). She hated it and suffered because the nicknames were Minnie or Minnie Ha Ha. Often, she used her middle name, Helen. When I was old enough to go shopping on my own and went in a store where the staff knew her, I would sometimes get confused momentarily since she had so many aliases!

My parents, Domenica and Nicholas Contino, had three kids—Roberta who died three days later; me, Rosalie, born a year later; and my brother, Robert or Bob, born two and half years later. My sister was named after the musical *Roberta,* written by Jerome Kern. My name came from the song, "Rosalie, My Darling," from the musical *Rosalie,* written by Cole Porter. My sister would have been Roberta or Robbie or Bobbie. I was called Rosalie, with Ro or Rosie ("Ugh," from me!). Of course, I had a song, "Rosalie, My Darling" from the show of the same name. Whenever a guy sang that song to me as I was dancing with him, I ran off the dance floor. I was mortified. I really hated my name. It wasn't until years later, when I got involved in musical theater at NYU and I heard those high sopranos singing, "Rosalie, where are you?" that I changed my attitude. Now, I love my name.

Bob got the best name of all. No one sang a song to him with his name in it because there weren't any at the time. He was named after a gorgeous actor, Robert Taylor. I don't think Bob ever forgot that he was named after a suave movie star whom all the girls swooned over. When he was a teenager, he tried to keep a debonair look about him. It's amazing how a name can shape a person. Shakespeare, to the contrary, said that some roses, as well as Rosalies, and even Bobs, blossom more sweetly with the right name.

I don't remember much of my brother as a kid, as I was too busy growing up and being cared for by two doting parents. Plus, I was the older one by two and a half years, and older siblings develop strategies for ignoring the younger ones. I know he was cute, chubby, and wore eyeglasses that usually hung crookedly on his face. One funny incident stands out in my mind. We were walking up to Bay Parkway, Brooklyn, and Mom was angry because Bob always swallowed the bubble gum instead of throwing it out. Mom informed him that all the gum would make a big bubble in his stomach and then what? He cried loudly all the way to Bay Parkway, the neighborhood shopping center in Brooklyn, holding his stomach. "See, it hurts already, right?" mother said. I guess he didn't swallow the gum anymore. At least, he didn't when Mom was around.

One unforgettable family story of the young Bob occurred when, as a small kid, he loved to follow the garbage men on their route up to the corner on his tricycle. My mother was mortified! She had aspirations for her son that most definitely did not include chasing garbage trucks down the street. She apologized to the sanitation workers and told them that she hoped he wasn't in their way. They told her that, on the contrary, they got a kick of having this kid following their route. They laughed and said that he would make a great supervisor. Mom thanked them for their kindness and waited until they were out of range before venting about their even *thinking* that such a remark was funny. One did not joke about the future of Domenica's children!

We were a close family and always together. As we got older and there were no more babysitters, my parents took us to the movies until we were old enough to be trusted on our own. I think my mother spent half of our life worried that we would be kidnapped. Can you imagine if we were young kids today? She would have had electronic tags attached to us. What could I say? My parents were older parents. Mom was in her late twenties and Dad's in his mid-thirties or late thirties when we were born, and were more cautious towards our well-being. I notice this with my friends who had kids at an older age and are just as fearful as my parents were. So be it. We always ate together. There were no teams to race out for practice and/or games and no meetings that would interrupt our daily routines. We talked to each other, and we listened to our favorite radio programs: *The Green Hornet, The Shadow, Amos and Andy, Life with Luigi*, and *The Lone Ranger*.

Then when television came on the scene, we watched the programs together in the living room. There was only one TV in the house at the time. Like most American families, we watched Ed Sullivan on Sunday nights who showcased many new entertainers. And, who could forget Milton Berle's zany antics, or Sid Ceasar and Imogene Coca's inventive and hilarious skits? What about Dinah Shore blowing us a kiss each week for the USA in her Chevrolet, or Loretta Young's calm demeanor as she, too, entered our living rooms costumed in sophisticated fashions each week? And there were the newer weekly TV shows, such as *Howdy Doody* for the kiddies, *Sky King,* for the teenagers, and for Mom there was *The Goldbergs*. Mom spent the entire show shaking her head and agreeing with Molly Goldberg's stance on life. Television even extended our religious obligations, I guess, since we were made to feel it was our duty to listen to the sermons of Bishop Robert Fulton Sheen.

It is amazing to look back on all the different ways television changed how we looked at things. To expand our horizons and hear and see what the outside world was contributing to mankind, we also watched Edward R. Murrow as he interviewed each guest. I sat mesmerized watching that cigarette smoke filter through the air as he spoke. For the first time, I became aware that the world could enter right into our living room, and we were affected by it.

Of course, when it came to sports, it was squatter's rights. Whoever got to the TV first got their choice of game, be it baseball or football. This was a way for Bobby to stay involved in sports as a kid, since, oddly enough, my brother did not play baseball, football, or basketball. Instead, he kept baseball scores and discussed or shared them with Dad or his friends. He was left-handed, and I think he was one of those kids who played ball the way left-handed people then wrote—sloppily.

Dad on the porch

Once, I remember when Mom, Dad, and I went to the park to play stickball. I always played in the streets with the kids on the block, but Bob couldn't hit the ball despite Dad's encouragement. He wasn't athletic; I was. I was always playing stickball or roller-skating in the streets, and playing guard, all five feet two inches of me, on two basketball teams—one in Fontbonne Hall Academy High School, and one in Saint Finbar's, our neighborhood church. He didn't.

We didn't travel far as my dad never owned a car, God forbid! (I realized recently, that Dad was an Electrical Engineer, worker for the Transit Authority, and the one making up the exams for the transit motormen. I guess he figured that if they passed his test, they had to be professional and good.) When my Uncle Frank, dad's brother, had time off from his patients, he would meet us at Central Park and drive upstate to Croton Lake Reservoir. We were appreciative because we had fun being away from the neighborhood! When my Dad had a vacation, he took us by bus to Coney Island, with our packed lunches and Cracker Jack as treats on the way home.

By the late 1950s, when my brother was a teenager, he was the most eligible bachelor on the block. From a chubby kid, he grew into a tall, willowy, cute guy. Every mother with an eligible daughter in the area made sure he was invited to a sweet sixteen, graduation, or special-something party. Parties were not elaborate affairs.

When we were younger, our parents would invite a few friends and relatives and have a birthday cake and soda. There were no "Sports Plus" venues to book spaces and pizza parties. Rather we played "Pin the Tail on the Donkey" in our homes. If you succeeded, you were given a simple prize—not any trip to Europe or pony rides in the backyard. Lastly, the best part was when we opened our gifts.

Of course, I'll always remember my sweet-sixteen birthday. My two friends came over and Mom surprised me with the "in" cake, a Sicilian specialty cake called Caserta, all covered with a glaze and glazed fruit. It was horrible.

"How could you do this to me?" I cried because I was mortified. My mother kept insisting that this was *the* cake to buy.

"What's wrong with you? It's the 'in' thing!" This was my Mom's favorite excuse. My brother's birthday was two years later. Somehow, I don't remember celebrating my brother's. He probably went out with his friends and probably didn't mention the day to them as he didn't like to call attention to himself. The only time I heard him react was when Mom reminded him every day about his braces.

"Bob, do you have your retainer on those teeth? I want those teeth to grow in straight and stay straight."

"Of course, Mom, I always have it with me." He would smile from afar. "See what a beautiful smile I have. Girls tell me that I have beautiful, straight teeth. Yes, they do. They don't like to date guys with crooked teeth."

We all knew that the minute he left the house, the retainer was placed neatly in his shirt pocket. He did not like wearing braces. That was probably the only time he made his own decisions and not our parents. I'm sure my parents asked him if he wanted anything special. Whatever it was, they worked it out between them, I really don't remember.

What a sharp contrast in comparison to the gala affairs teenagers are treated today in local catering halls, complete with screaming deejays and blasting disco, hip hop, or rap music, not to mention colorful Mylar balloons decorating color-coordinated tables and six-foot heroes aptly called "The

Kitchen Sink," an invention to accommodate the growing demands for ethnic foods! Also, there were no options of a trip to Disney World or a cruise to their favorite Caribbean island with their friends with cell phone appendages attached to their ears or text messaging to report to those left on shore. Naturally, the mommies and daddies (one or the other or both, another rarity) were in tow, not only to foot the bills, but to happily brag of the privilege to share in the experiences of their children's latest endeavors based their own financial offerings, also known as a severe case of *credit-carditis*.

Then, we all watched Dick Clark's *American Bandstand* to keep up with the latest rock and roll hits and dance crazes. This entertainment added to simple innocent basement parties where teenagers meet to enjoy themselves over Coca-Cola or Pepsi and pretzels or potato chips to talk, to flirt, and to hear the latest rage in music—rhythm and blues (especially Elvis Presley, Bob's choice then), or early rock and roll music, or play the most adventurous "Spin the Bottle" and hope for the best.

I lost count of how many times I took the bus to Bay Parkway to buy Bob the latest record or album for that special "new" girl, along with the "special" wrapping paper, "colorful" ribbon, and a "special" birthday card that really "identified" him. No matter how I protested to my parents, I was informed that this was *my* obligation. My parents ignored my pleas no matter how hard I cried and wheedled.

Mom at home.

"That's the least you could do for your brother. You're the older one and should know better."

Once they said that, the guilt set in and I walked humbly to the corner and waited for the bus. If I was in the mood, I walked the two miles and window-shopped. I grew to love the Rainbow Shop, Darene's, and Phillip's Dress Shoppe, and forgot all about the real shopping mecca, A&S, Downtown Brooklyn, the store that had a wonderful reputation, though, in a pinch, if nobody else had the merchandise, A&S would, and it saved you a trip to the city.

The Rainbow Shop was a chain, but Darene's and Phillip's were the *crème de la crème* of Bay Parkway. If you lived in this neighborhood and you needed something exquisite, these were the *places* to shop. My mother was a steady customer. At least, the trip shouldn't be wasted since I reported back what the latest was in the windows.

Bob and I had the same opportunities to be successful in life. Although I was older, I wasn't allowed to stay out as late as he was at the same age. I didn't agree with my parents' decision, but I didn't have a choice. I felt that it wasn't fair and complained that he had more rights than I did. My parents told me to stop complaining and to be thankful that they cared enough about us to set these guidelines. Huh?

My parents showed no favoritism regarding high school. The education for girls in public high schools was changing. From my parents' hard work and sacrifice (How often do I still hear the trumpets playing when I say this line.), they were able to send me, whether I agreed or not, to Fontbonne Hall Academy in Bay Ridge, Brooklyn, the best Catholic high school for girls then and now. It's a great location because it overlooked Gravesend Bay, and now, the Verrazano Bridge.

At first, I was not a happy camper because *none* of my friends went there. They were attending the public schools instead. Aunt Rose, my godmother and Mom's best friend since childhood, spoke high praise for Fontbonne's education and the quality of the students who went there. Her oldest daughter went there, and now, one who was my age was going. The following year, the friend, with whom I grew up, attended Fontbonne as well. I made a lot of new friends. Many of us from that class went to Fordham University and majored in education. Today, I am still close to one friend after all those years. Yet, I wasn't thrilled that it was an all-girls school. I had to listen to friends who spoke about the gorgeous guys on the football teams or basketball teams who sat next to them in classes in the public high schools. But all was not lost! There was still a chance to mingle.

On Wednesday nights, Saint Bernadette had a social with cookies, soda, and music, and on Fridays, it was Saint Finbar's turn. We didn't have the teams to root for, but there were guys to meet, dance, and date. My friends and I also expanded our social life by roller-skating at the Bay Ridge Roller Rink on Friday nights. I couldn't wait to wear a new sweater with the latest Peter Pan collar or latest skating outfit that Mom made for me. We waited anxiously for the couples' dance to see who would pick us to skate with them. It was fun, but the only guy I remember was the one who quit school at thirteen to become a butcher. When I told my parents, they were just as amazed as I was because leaving school so young just wasn't done anymore.

When it came to Bob, he was allowed to attend the school of his choice. He refused to go to a Catholic high school for boys because he felt the boys were "sissies." What a laugh—like he was such a fighter! Off to Lafayette High School he went for his four years, with the friends he grew up with—the school he was zoned to go to. When it came time for college, I chose to go to Fordham University as a day student; he opted for night school at the newly accredited Pace College, as well as Baruch Business School (CUNY) because he wanted cash in his pocket. Why not?

At that moment in life, he seemed to be the pilot of his soul and the captain of his destiny. He had looks, youth, and a supportive family. He had friends, and he had girls who cooed over him. Why should he not have felt that the toughest thing he would ever have to decide was exactly which way he would get to make his mark on the world?

Little did any of us know what the future held in store.

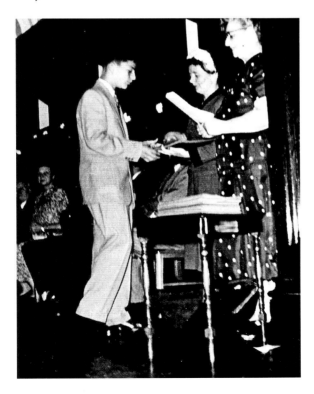

Graduation from the 8th grade from PS 163 BK, 1954

The Shock of a Friendship

Fast forward a few decades...

I am sorry that Bob's life was not as fruitful as I thought it should have been. I was sorry that at the peak of his life, when all was going well, he was cut down by a mental illness that changed the course of his life forever. I am heartbroken that not one friend stayed with him through his troubles. Ironically, the isolation Bob must have felt was brought home to me a few years ago when one of my friendships, one of forty-two-years standing, was irretrievably lost because of how this woman treated Bob.

For many years, my brother refused to go to weddings because he thought they were silly. I told my friends and family, "Don't bother inviting him, he'll only say 'no.'" That being said, there are always exceptions. One exception that I expected to be made was for the wedding of a friend's daughter who was my godchild. For years, I spent Christmas Eve with her and her family. When my mother died, she insisted on my father and brother joining them as well, since we were all family. After all, we're Italians, right? Bob received the same invitation when Dad passed away.

I was so excited. *Jenner was getting married. Her mother, a long-time friend from college, was also excited. The envelope had my name written in fancy calligraphy. I thought it odd that only my name was on the envelope, but ignored the omission. I opened the envelope and read the wedding announcement that was neatly embossed and printed on quality paper. I smiled. It was very stylish, and I loved their taste. Or at least, I did until I realized that the invitation had only my name on it. I was dumbfounded. What happened to Bob being family all of a sudden?

I called my friend immediately, and with tears already seeping into my voice, I asked her why.

"Why what?" she asked calmly.

"Why? After all," I said, "you invited him for Christmas Eve every year so why not the wedding? In fact, you insisted and assured me that it was okay because we were family."

"Oh, one thing has nothing to do with the other. Look, we have to invite lots of people to the wedding, and I am running out of space. I don't even know some of them"

"Huh? Or better still, he didn't fit the *type* of person to be seen at *the* wedding."

"Look, I have to go. There's a lot of things that have to be done."

I was devastated for weeks—I mean, after all, we were friends for forty-two years! What was that she assured me about over and over again? That Bob will be okay, that there was nothing to be ashamed of, that mental illness was just a sickness like the measles? If anyone thought differently, well then, they were just ignorant! Now, I guess he wasn't good enough to be a guest. Why? Because he didn't fit the norm of looking the way wedding guests should look? However, I am my mother's daughter. I went to the wedding all dolled up. And then never spoke to her again!

Rule # 1: Look the best that you can look. I knew everyone would be in black except the bride, of course. I bought myself a beautiful, fine, pale lemon, three-piece outfit. I put on the biggest smile and danced the night away. I absolutely enjoyed myself as much as I could. At the end of the evening, I bid good night to everyone, and wished the bride and groom a good life.

As I think back though, I laugh, so much for being Italian—from the land of love and compassion—right? So much for friendship and family, in the end it is total bullshit. It's bad enough that Bob lost all his friends who were friends since kindergarten when he got sick. And now, this?

A Son's Song; A Family's Pain

B ob was a handicapped person. Quite often, I forgot that he was a man with "special needs," and became utterly focused on that other fact of life—that he was also my annoying little brother, Bob. I remember clearly those times when he made a mistake, or we needed more money added to the joint checking account. In his mind, it was my fault—as it was *my job* to add to the coffers. Bob automatically shirked his responsibilities to discuss, correct, or to add, and denied all by going to bed. How much of this was illness and how much was my brother's true personality, I suppose I will never know. But then again, this is one thing I have learned—there is no bright dividing line between illness and health. And it is precisely because the line is vague that things can be manipulated and recast to suit whoever cares to make an issue of something.

On May 11, 2001, I received a phone call from *Jason, my brother's boss, regarding Bob's vacation time from the mailroom where he worked.

"Yes, I wish he would take his vacation time as soon as possible. You know, your brother has outlived his usefulness." He continued in a manner-of-fact tone, "We want to free up some space. We are not a babysitting service. We want him out. We don't need him to sleep here every day. Have you found a home to put him in? He's suffering! Can't you see that? Have you started the papers yet?"

I sat there, stunned, holding the phone away, and did not know what to say. He didn't even call my brother by name; just kept referring to him as "he"…just, "he." I needed time to catch my breath and asked Jason if I could call him back.

When I called back a few minutes later, *Eddy, the nice boss, answered.

"You know what it is," he said gently. "We want him to pack it in. Bob's been working almost forty years. It's time for him to enjoy his life. He'll get a good package, plus a bonus. If you want to find out exactly, call *Joel Bassano, the main boss, and he'll tell you more."

From what I gathered from Eddy, they were afraid to send Bob out to deliver letters to other sources because they noticed that he limped more frequently and walked slowly across the street. (It wasn't until Bob retired, that he was diagnosed with an arthritic hip.) If he got hit by a car, they felt responsible. Instead, they let him sit at a desk or table in the afternoon. However, I mentioned to Eddy that, a few weeks earlier, Bob complained to me that he and the others sat at a table in the afternoon because they had nothing to do. When Bob was younger, he sat; now he slept. Eddy said that it was true. Because of e-mails and Fed Ex, etc., there were fewer letters to be delivered and fewer clerks hired for this job. Of course, New York City budget cuts were included in the new financial picture of this department. I appreciated his concern and explanation as I have had many pleasant conversations with Eddy over the years.

Eddy had a good sense of humor, especially regarding Bob's chain-smoking habit.

They used to hide the cigarettes from Bob to help him cut down on his addiction. At lunch time, Bob, of course, would buy another pack. At the end of the day, they returned the pack. I wasn't aware of this as I could never figure out why he had so many open packs of cigarettes in his coat or jackets. He blew it off with his usual quirky answer.

"Stay out of my pockets!" he'd yell, when I asked why he had so many packs.

I hung up with Eddy on a positive note, as I usually did with him. He gave me the number of the Joel Bassano, Bob's boss of the department and I promised to call. Now I had to figure out how my brother could whittle down the 180 vacation days he had coming to him. Bob hated to take off because he insisted they needed him at work. One or two weeks a year was the best he could "afford." However, I couldn't forget the harsh, stinging, sarcastic words ringing in my ears from Jason.

"*He has outlived his usefulness!*" I was mortified. I was told for years that, "He is a good man." "Bobby is a dedicated worker who gets along with everybody." "Everybody loves him to death!" Oh? Really? "Did his work include sleeping on the job?"

I guess my job now was to convince him to retire and have long talks with him to do just that.

"At your salary," I said, "they can hire two for the price of one." I paused to let that sink in, to allow him to feel that he was a man who was worth two other men. "You're sixty-one years old, you have the time, and the buyout is good. You won't get a deal better that this. Just go for it."

My brother was a rare breed—a conscientious worker who refused to take his vacation days. Persuading him to retire now became a major project for me because this job was also his life.

"I have to think about it," Bob said.

My brother was a people person. To deliver the mail from floor to floor and to meet and greet everyone was his main contact each day. I begged him to start taking days off.

"Think of it, we can take day trips to different places. We can eat out in "exotic places." I changed my tone of voice to convince him.

"I have to think about it," Bob said again.

"Good. Think very hard and be practical. Think of the money you'll receive for sitting home and not taking car service to the station or racing to catch the buses and trains or in all kinds of weather. You'll get a great package. I mean how many people want to work after sixty?"

"I'll let you know," he said.

Now that I had the irresistible force in play, it was time to work on the immovable object—putting the papers in order for Bob's retirement.

A Decision To Be Made

The next morning, I called Joel Bassano, Bob's boss, and asked him what package Bob was entitled to. I also informed him that I would convince my brother to retire. The powers that be suggested he stay home and continue using his vacation days. On July 20, I met with the rep from human resources for copies of his work history and to go over what he was entitled to upon retirement. She was insistent that he sign the forms at once. I wasn't happy with that, but I agreed to go over the information with him. Since I had been a teacher, the UFT is one of our final stops before retirement. I called his union and asked if members had final consultations with them as well. They did. We had an appointment on September 20 at the union headquarters.

The paychecks still came in every two weeks, via Airborne Express, until the middle of August. Then—nothing at all! I called the office and was informed that since payroll didn't hear from him for weeks, my brother was considered in limbo. Didn't they tell him (me) to take the days as vacation time? Basically those "vacation days" were translated as "recuperation time." It would have been nice or logical if someone sent a professional letter stating the rules of the game, the procedure, rather than waiting for the next letter or phone calls. I had loads of information on my brother's medical and retirement benefits but nothing on office regulations, only hearsay. Most people who work in a mail room are usually handicapped in one way or another. What if they lived alone and had no one to ask or represent them? What happens then? Here, I thought I had everything under control and didn't. As a teacher and member of the UFT, I received information constantly regarding days, vacation time, medical leaves, and the like. Teachers were allotted ten days a year. If you use more, you were docked or it was deducted from the next year. This city agency was for the birds.

The rule was written somewhere I guess, that if Bob was going to get paid for the remainder of his vacation days, he needed a doctor's note. When I looked at the doctor's note, I flipped out because I knew my brother had hypertension, uncontrollable high blood pressure, and congestive heart failure—via smoking. Why the hell wasn't I told that there was not much improvement despite the new medications? I would have drugged him and driven him to a hospital to be cured. Without further ado, I did as I was told. I called the doctor, picked up the note, and sent it Priority Mail to the office.

I received a call from my brother's office that the doctor's note did not have a date on it. I called the doctor's office again, picked up another note from the doctor, and asked the nurse if she could fax it to my brother's office. She replied that she didn't know if she could fit it into her schedule. I thanked her, took the doctor's note, and faxed it from my house. Immediately I got a phone call from Eddy. Not good enough because it was not faxed from the doctor's office. Back to square one, folks, or how to keep the salary away from the worker. The powers that be also needed more information about my brother's medical problems from the doctor in order to get his back pay. I called the doctor's office again. The problem was resolved after three more "agains" and the proper medical information was accepted.

I cancelled going to Minneapolis because I feared I would find my brother dead when I come back. I didn't need any guilt trips because, now that we were both home, I saw his health did not improve. I wasn't happy knowing that he wasn't in good physical condition. It was hard to fathom how I saw his health changed drastically from one day to the other, even though he was home resting without any stress to confront him. We were at the doctor's office constantly because I could see there was no improvement. He always looked one step before the grave.

At the same time, I was trying to make it as a playwright. So, all the while I was working on Bob and his retirement, I mailed every play I wrote to every theater that might option it for a production or to agents who would consider me a *find*.

I don't know what stamina Bob had to walk two to three blocks every day to the nearest restaurant or diner for breakfast. When he came home, he would tell me that he saw Raffi and Palma—two deceased cousins. I was freaking out. He was smoking and coughing constantly and could hardly walk. No matter what I said, he pretended that I must have meant someone else and not him. It didn't pay to hide the cigarettes because what was to stop him from walking out to the nearest store and buying another pack?

Now, my brother could not fit into his shoes. From an 11M, his feet swelled to a 13E. The only problem was where to find men's shoes that size. Most stores in the area did not have a request for them and therefore didn't stock them. Bob refused to wear sneakers because whether at home or at work, he thought they were unprofessional. Finally, when we went shopping at Macy's in Staten Island, we found a pair that Bob approved of in style and size and purchased them. Still, he looked terrible and his feet were still swollen.

Most of the time, my brother went to his therapist by himself. She was a wonderful, caring, human being, and very interested and concerned for my brother's well-being. She worked for the New York State Mental Health Services that Bob was part of since he was released from Pilgrim State Hospital in 1963. As in the past, in 1980, I called to make them aware about Dad's failing health. I encouraged Bob to make extra appointments when he felt he had to talk to her. He did. On August 20, 2001, I went to see her myself because I was at my wits' end dealing with Bob's failing health.

"What are you doing? Why are you handling this by yourself?" she said. "He should be getting proper care, and that's in the hospital, not at home. He looks terrible."

"I promised my parents I would take care of him," I said. "You know, teachers are taught always to handle situations by themselves. Once you're in the classroom, it's family and you are a total unit, no matter what the situation is, unless it's truly, truly serious. Bob thinks he's going to die if he goes to a hospital."

"And if he dies in the house, how will you feel?"

"Terrible"

"Go home and call an ambulance."

I did.

The two EMS drivers arrived at the house, and I whispered that my brother was not going to be easy to convince to go to the hospital.

"Stay in the kitchen," they answered. "Let us do our job. He won't be the first to say 'no' and he won't be the last." I did as suggested. What followed was a comedy scene.

"Well, Sir, what seems to be the problem? Your sister says she's concerned for your health."

"Yes," Bob answered, "but, I'm not. I hate hospitals. She," he glared at me, "and *they* make up stories that I am sick. And I know for sure that I'm not."

Without discussing the issue any further, they gave him a choice of five hospitals—Saint Vincent's Hospital in Manhattan or Staten Island, Lutheran, Victory Memorial, or Maimonides in Brooklyn. As they spoke in normal tones, without getting excited and in a matter-of-fact tone, Bob went through why he didn't want the four of them. He noted that Saint Vincent's Hospital in Manhattan was out because it would take me too long to drive in; he feared that I wouldn't show up to visit him. (Very considerate, I might add.) Three hospitals in Brooklyn were out because he had been in each of them and wanted nothing to do with them. He didn't want to hear what the doctors had to say or needed, as well as so many tests and x-rays. He couldn't figure out why they took so many MRIs of his head. They understood his complaint, but since they didn't know his medical history, they couldn't give him an honest answer. I thank these men even today.

After much discussion with EMS and five hospital choices later, my brother agreed to go to Saint Vincent's in Staten Island. He was admitted with pneumonia, hypertension, congestive heart failure, emphysema, asthma, and cellulitis. As the EMS people left, they suggested that I take my time going there to give the hospital some time to admit Bob for fear that once he sees me and hasn't been admitted, he will create a scene and come home with me.

And this is how we celebrated Labor Day in 2001.

Sleep at Last for a While

For the first time in weeks, I slept through the night because Bob was in safe hands. Of course, the joke was that he told the nurse he only smoked three to four cigarettes per day for over forty years.

"Beautiful," he said, "beautiful."

I laughed when he told me the story.

"Moron! Don't you think they see that your hands are yellow from your three to four packs a day? Do you think they are idiots?"

"Gee, leave it to you to tell my secrets."

"I didn't. You did. You left evidence, my dear brother, you left evidence."

"Uh-oh, okay."

Bob's major complaint each day was that the aides "thrashed his body to and fro" and his body was not in any condition to take it.

"Please tell them to leave my poor old body alone," he begged.

"Oh, please," I said, "they have to wash you every day. Stop saying you're an old man. You are in the prime of your new life—end of your work and the beginning of retirement. Think of it! No more waiting for call service to pick you up or take you home to or from the station. No more waiting for the trains or the buses. Get a life!"

"I would if I didn't have to be here. It's boring. There's no one to talk to. It's like a ghost town. Who can we call? All the patients are gone except me."

"It's Labor Day weekend, get it?"

"Oh," he said sadly, "why did we pick this place?"

"You wanted Staten Island," I reminded him, "not me."

The hospital personnel were very kind to him. Since he was the only one in his room, they let him sit in the hallway where people greeted him as they passed by. Bob cheered up and survived very nicely as each passerby spoke to him for a few minutes. The aides were very sweet to him, and many times would pat his cheek and asked if he needed anything. He let them shave him gladly as he didn't want to anymore. He complained that there was something with his hands or he couldn't hold the razor right and/or he didn't want a shaver. I just attributed this to "for the want of services," as usual. When I visited him, he asked me to give them a tip. At first the aides were hesitant and embarrassed, but we insisted. Somehow, Bob had that magic aura about him that drew people to help him, and receiving a tip was not part of their services.

One incident I remember so clearly was when I asked to have a psychologist or psychiatrist speak with Bob. I also insisted being present in the room as I wasn't looking to have him roped into a psych ward that was part of the services of this hospital setting. I worked with enough professionals in the field that I know that certain tell-tale signs would warrant that decision. I wanted to hear what the doctor had to say or ask, and more importantly, how Bob responded. What I got was a young man probably on his first day on the job. He was impeccably dressed in a nice dark suit with a white shirt and small-patterned tie. After introducing himself, the conversation went as follows:

"With her you live?" was his first question.

"Yes," Bob looked at me as he answered.

"With you he lives?" I nodded, my head trying to keep a straight face.

He asked Bob a lot of questions pertaining to snakes, and if he saw them at work. Bob answered adamantly, "No!" He admitted that he saw them at home. Oh, how I remembered those days when he would yell, "Snakes! Snakes!"

I just stared at him and asked, "What is the matter?"

"Who me? Nothing! Nothing at all! You're just imagining things!"

I thought the session went well and appreciated the way he spoke and the respect he showed my brother.

Often, when you go from one doctor to another, and the doctor is aware that he is not dealing with a person with a full deck, he can be brusque, which was very upsetting to me. I complained to my friends about their attitudes.

"Look! It's human nature. They all can't adore their patients." My friends comforted me, adding, "They have their concerns also…and fear the patients may harm them."

"Bobby wouldn't do that!" I argued.

"Yes, but they don't know him," was the usual response. "Be realistic. A new doctor does not know the nature of his problems."

I made sure I was always present with each doctor's visit.

At one point, the doctor asked questions, and Bob and I just looked at him. Suddenly, the "verb" followed. Good grief! What if I wasn't there or if it was a different type of patient? That person would really be scratching his head and wondering which end was up.

Afterwards, I spoke to one of the doctors and suggested that he was a nice professional who needed to take a refresher course in English. Despite the "missing verbs" I had a good feeling about the session. The doctor *also* felt that Bob was okay, and there was no cause for alarm.

"This young man has to make friends with verbs or he will be outside looking in," I said to Bob when he left. We shared a good laugh over this incident.

Another payday went by with no check in the mail. In the past, I relied on my godmother, Palma, who was alive at the time, to help me out in emergencies. She was a cousin who was my godmother, my mother's confidant, and now mine. There was an eight-year difference in their age. Now, I had to rely on me only. It still didn't click that I was going to be the chief cook and bottle washer of this experience. I also knew that if I called payroll one more goddamn time, I would scream like a lunatic and resolve nothing. But I counted slowly to ten and made the call. The payroll person we requested was off that day, and I asked to have her call me the next day. She did and was informed that the doctor's papers were submitted and my brother would get paid shortly. The situation was out of her hands.

Labor Day became the holiday I liked the least. Years before, when I went to the Hamptons, I found out that my dad had vertigo that weekend. My mother called my uncle, the doctor, who rushed over immediately. When he told Dad to show him his heart, Dad put his hand in his pj top and pretend to hold his heart in his hand. Uncle Frank was not amused and asked my mother how she had stood his humor.

Once again, I would spend Labor Day for medical problems and emergencies—now going back and forth to Staten Island for Bob—but it was worth it. After being in the hospital four days, Bob stated:

"I'm awake all day. I feel good. Why do you think that is?"

"You're not smoking nor on any medications that you were on previously, Bob," and to myself I said, "*Thank you, God!*"

"Let's go home."

"Please, it's not that easy."

On September 6, my brother was discharged from the hospital with new medications, a walker, a visiting nurse, a physical therapist—the works. They evaluated his medical situation. He needed an aide to come in daily to tend to, and massage his legs (cellulitis) to heal better, and have more exercise. I hired an aide, out of pocket, to take care of him for five days a week, four hours each day. Since he couldn't walk the three or four blocks to his favorite eating places, the aide or me cooked for him or he ordered from the local deli or pizza place. Bless my brother, he never missed a meal and absolutely loved service.

Bob was supposed to be on a low salt diet. I knew I could cook salt-free for me, but him? Before, it was ridiculous even to think about it. Now, he was home full time, and I had more control over what to feed him. The fast foods he frequented in the city were now to be a thing of the past. Most importantly, he hadn't smoked in ten days. Whoopee! I had great confidence that he would stop forever and live to a ripe old age. Also, the last hospital stay scared him momentarily. My brother would never admit that this was a wise decision.

"Ah, for the taste of a cigarette," or "Ah, is that the smell of a cigarette? I wonder where it's coming from." He would torture me with that line from time to time. I knew he wanted me to open the door to see who was passing to bum a cigarette. The threat I hung over his head was that if he did, I would sign him in an old man's nursing home with old nurses and no blondes to take care of him! I wasn't kidding!

On September 7, there was once again no paycheck. I called payroll. I was switched to five different office divisions of payroll only to hear, "Who?" over and over like a midnight chorus of owls. No one had heard of my brother. Was he fired? Was he a temp? He was not listed on the payroll. However, the last person I spoke to promised to get back to me. It never happened. I called later, and his boss stated that he would get back to me. It never happened.

Needless to say, what occurred on September 11 of that year needs no explanation. We sat in limbo like the rest of the world as we waited and watched with eyes glued to the television for the next set of events that unfolded before our very eyes. Although the buildings went down in Lower Manhattan, we live twenty minutes away by car in Brooklyn. That was close enough and scary. There was the smell of death, whenever we opened the backdoor, for months.

Back and Forth—the Seesaw Effect

I was scheduled to do two workshops during this crazy time of trying to land Bob into retirement. One was conducting a creative writing workshop in Minneapolis, for Pi Lambda Theta, the educational honor society that I belonged to, and another was a workshop on the contribution of Percy Anderson, a turn-of-the-century costume designer for the American Alliance for Theater in Education (AATE) Conference in San Diego the following week. I was very excited about the PLT session because it was for adults who swore they never wrote or could write yet; they were willing to sit in on my class. In the fifteen minutes I gave them, I ask them to write their thoughts on such topics as "being a two-hundred-year-old tree," or "if you had to start all over again, what would you want to be or wish for," or "what made you decide on an important decision in your life." The previous sessions were successful and amazing for me and the group. In retrospect, I was sorry I didn't collect them and have them printed as souvenirs for each to keep. If nothing else, it would have been a nice publishing credit if they needed one, since most of them were educators whose job descriptions required such. I cancelled based on what would follow soon after. Realistically speaking, I had to cancel attending because Bob's health was more important. There would always be more conferences to attend.

Bobby was on new medications to reduce his high blood pressure, high cholesterol, emphysema, and asthma due to a heavy smoking habit. They did. One of the side effects was that he slept a lot at home in his favorite chair, the Queen Anne chair. I called the doctor.

"So? At least his health is improving," the doctor said.

Duh? I thought to myself.

I called Bob's union to confirm the appointment for September 20 to meet with his pension board union rep for final consultation before retiring. They knew who he was and had his files. Why them and not the other offices?

The office was located at the Marriott Hotel in Downtown Brooklyn where all city workers met with reps for their final meetings. The rep was terrific. I found out everything I needed to know including what numbers to call for his paycheck.

I had copies of Bob's important work facts, and the rep figured out what his retirement pension was going to be for his thirty-nine years of service plus a two-year bonus. He knew when he was going to get his salary reinstated!

The rep suggested I call payroll office. All I could think of was, "Again?" and for what? He suggested that I convince my brother to retire. This was for sure, I told them, even if I had to tie him up from 10:00 A.M. to 6:00 P.M.

Bob sat there noncommitted, just listening. The rep suggested that Bob become a volunteer.

"My sister is a volunteer, not me," he answered bluntly.

The rep suggested that he take a computer course, a cooking course, or a movie course.

"My sister loves to sit at her computer all day. I like to eat out or order from Ravioli Fair or Pizza Den. We have Cablevision," Bob answered curtly. "I don't need to leave the house for a movie. It's all on the TV. All I have to do is press the button and flip the channels. End of story!"

On the way home, we fought like cats and dogs because he still refused to admit that it was time to enjoy his retirement.

"Why must I retire? I have a good rating. There's nothing in my file that says I don't. Just because you did, it doesn't mean I have to!" he said over and over. He was right.

I saw the tears welling up in his eyes and hoped he couldn't see them in mine.

"That's not the point! Look, you can go to Europe, China, Russia, a cruise—anywhere you like. Think of the money you will receive and the two-year bonus to boot! Whammo! Think of all the places I've been to, and you can see go to more than I have. You are free after thirty-nine years on the job! Think about it!"

That's really the problem, I thought, *getting him to think about it.*

"I have. I am an American-born citizen who likes to stay in America. I don't want to go anywhere else. End of story! What CD is playing in this car—Rod Stewart? We should have visited J&R Records for CDs."

At home, I called his therapist who promised to give him a list of recreational options once he retired. I wasn't too keen on these places because the recreational places she suggested were for people with disabilities—less than or more severe than his. I felt Bob should have a more normal setting and not one to remind him of his own problems. I think my teaching days were reminders of the caliber of the special education students I was used to seeing in the schools in which I taught. Without him saying so, I always felt that Bob was not that stupid to realize the group that he would be socializing with. I gave him the information the therapist suggested.

"Are they nearby?" he asked.

"Some of them are."

"How would I get there?"

"I guess by bus or train," I added enthusiastically. "Think of it as a chance to meet and be with people. You don't have to sit in the house day after day because you're retired. You can also get lunch."

"You know, when you get on an idea, you never give up. I know you. I'll let you know when I want the list."

"Aye, aye, Sir. Am awaiting for your answer," I answered kiddingly.

However, Bob refused to deal with her suggestions as he did with retirement and never mentioned it again.

Then I resumed the *quest for back pay*. Oh, where, oh, where were those checks? I was like a woman obsessed now—even more so than my brother for the degrading way I had to beg for what was his. On October 9, I called payroll at the Broadway office that referred me to timekeeping, which referred me to human resources that redirected me back to timekeeping. I spoke to the clerk and explained the damn frustrating, perplexing situation to her. Timekeeping promised to call me back. *Dead zone*, thought I. But I was wrong; she did. I asked her why she called me back. She was taken aback. She replied, "I told you I would."

"Well," said I, "nobody else has," and explained my frustration since August 16.

My brother's records were not available because they were stuck in the building across from the World Trade Center. Now, Bob's records were purged because he was on sick leave and trying to retire. Why weren't they on more than one computer terminal? Why not ask the union for a set? It sure seemed as though they had everyone's records.

After more ado or heated detail, on October 16, 2001, Bob and I drove to the Brooklyn Marriott Hotel again to sign the retirement papers. He would get thirty-nine years plus two years bonus plus sixty some odd days left. *Good grief*, I thought! *He still had days left?* I was shocked at the few forms he had to fill out. The union rep asked why I was surprised. I said the UFT teachers filled out reams of forms and then some. He reminded us to get the retiree's form for medical benefits.

On October 28, I called back again. Good news! Bob would get back pay dating from August 16. The paper work was almost done. I promised the clerk roses if my brother got his back pay.

"Don't be silly," she said and laughed, "I'm only doing my job."

I collected his first check November 6 after 10:30 A.M. My brother wrote a letter permitting me to pick up his check. At least, one of us should be sufficient to represent him to collect his way overdue salary. When I signed in and identified myself, all remembered my brother and wished him well and hoped that he would visit them soon. I rode the elevator to the third floor office and introduced myself.

One young lady remembered Bob because he always told her she had beautiful Spanish hair. On the other hand, he nagged me that mine was too short or too long or that it never looked good. I promised to tell Bob that she missed him, and when he comes in, she will take him to lunch. She had fond memories of Bob as he was always sweet and polite. I was elated that Bob did our parents proud. Whenever I met anyone who knew him, they always commented on how sweet and polite he was. When introduced to the office staff, they asked if Bob missed the office. I said, "Yes, but he missed his paycheck first and the office second." They laughed. His paycheck reflected August 16 to November 6. I sent a bouquet of roses to the young payroll clerk who was so helpful. After all, I promised.

A young African-American man walked in with the mail. His name was *Allan. Aha, my brother's friend. After I introduced myself, we had a short conversation, and he moved on to deliver mail to other floors. Next answer: Bob will get paid next week on November 27. The check awaits him. Bring ID. My brother came with me because he wanted to see Allan. We went to get his anxiously awaited paycheck and to visit the third floor office.

The staff greeted my brother with much affection and love. He greeted them cordially. I knew he's being nice because he's anxious to see the check. It's half of his usual pay. Christ! Here we go again! No! We were assured that since he was officially retired, he will get lump sum in one month. Let's hope it's before the end of the year so he can set up a tax deferred account and save some money. We left and walked across to J&R Records, Bob's favorite store. He always managed to find bargains each time he walked in. If buying CDs gave him comfort as a way to start his retirement, I'd gladly oblige.

"You made me retire. May I buy some new CDs so that I can listen to them at home, little sister?" he asked.

"Of course, why would I argue about that?"

We did and drove home. Days later, the payroll clerk and I discussed why Bob was inadvertently taken off the payroll. The clerk replied that this was a common problem. A woman employee in another department was sick for two weeks and they threw her off the payroll.

"Oh, they considered him in limbo because he hasn't gotten back to them," one boss said weeks later. I reminded the gentleman that he was told to take his vacation days which did not include a doctor's note.

Maybe that was the time I was taking my brother back and forth to the doctor because the medication wasn't working as I thought it should. Bob was sleeping too many hours and could hardly function. I shuddered and feared, what if he fell asleep on the train and woke up in a seedy part of the city? Better still, was it because he was a man with *special needs,* and they figured they could pull the wool over his eyes? Was it because I questioned his benefits and I wanted to meet with the union first to clarify some information?

How many in his department can defend themselves in this situation? I thought it very suspicious that human resources insisted on July 20 that he sign his retirement papers as soon as possible. Everyone was sweet the minute I asked about his retirement benefits. And when he didn't sign immediately, the phone from his office stopped ringing immediately prior to September 11. Was their attitude really one of as in the words of one of his bosses:

"Have you found a home to put your brother away in yet? We're not running a babysitting service here. We need to free up the space."

However, as I think back, maybe I was being unrealistic. I noticed, after meeting and talking with different people in his office, that if Bob wasn't well-liked, they could have easily replaced him as we have all seen done to employees in our own working environments. They saw him every day for years, for more hours than I did. For me, he came home, ate, watched TV, and went to bed. They noticed they weren't working with what Bobby used to be, and wanted a fresher, and healthier person who could breathe easier, walk faster than he now do, and paid less. Also, he was off their conscience, and they could rest easier.

I also realized that he was handicapped and worked for every dime he had coming to him. I was adamant that he get his due. I was also proud of the fact that he functioned and lasted over thirty-nine years on the job. I guess, in a sense, it was closure for me because I was able to resolve these issues for him before he moved on. I thought of the kids we worked with, and how often we had to go to bat for them for different problems. This was different because this was for my brother.

Retirement Can Be a Bitter Pill to Swallow

After over thirty-nine years on the job, retirement was a hard pill for Bob to swallow because he had nowhere to go or nothing to do. Presently, his day consisted of going to work, stopping by J&R Records for CDs located across from his office at City Hall in Manhattan, and coming home. When he was younger, he started a collection of Lionel trains—every part from A to Z. Each Christmas, he and Dad spent hours setting up the train board the size of a dining room table in between the dining room and the living room. For hours on end, Mom and I heard:

"Christ! Hold this will ya!"

"Where are the pliers or the wire cutter or the scissors, or the tape?"

"Have no fear, Dad! Here it is."

Dad was the electrical engineer, so this was a piece of cake for him. Bob, on other hand, wasn't but was a quick learner. After all, he paid for these trains and was quite finicky in making sure each track was connected correctly and each train worked. Once properly set up, we invited friends or neighbors with kids to see the Lionel trains in action, especially the locomotive puffing away as it made its way round and round the track. We always had a lot of fun cheering each time it did. As Dad got older and was not up to par to set up the trains, Bob lost interest, too. They were stored in the garage until further notice.

Presently, Bob had no hobbies that would get him out of the house to meet and be with people with the same interests. Who else did he have besides me? A few of my friends and relatives who had not forsaken him, I guess. Better them, than no one. When he was hospitalized in 1963 due to a physical breakdown and not a mental breakdown, then Dad said it was a *slight* case of schizophrenia.

"The tip of the iceberg," he used to say each time we spoke about it.

How slight was slight? Consider the worst of the scenarios.

Bob lost all his friends because people were afraid of him or took him off their list of friends. At that time, it was assumed that if you had a breakdown, it was a mental one. You were someone not to be associated with for fear that you, this patient, would harm them. Being in a mental institution was being in a psycho ward, with crazies screaming and yelling or getting beaten up. People judged you because there was not that much known about the disease. Bob and his friends were together since kindergarten, and at that time were in college or recent graduates. Being educated didn't count then, and supposedly, it's one step ahead of stupidity regarding people with mental disease. Being sympathetic and compassionate would have been nice, too, but that was all too rare then.

When many of my friends were patients of hypnotists, therapists, psychologists, psychiatrists, or, to say the least, psychotherapists for one psychological problem or another, I didn't throw them on a "don't call" list. I was happy that they had sought professional help to resolve the issues that were bothering them. Then, there was no public awareness of what mental illness was really about.

Often today, when I see a program on the topic, they are usually concerned with the most severe forms of schizophrenia, especially in young adults. Then there are the all too familiar with those blazing headlines of junior high or high school students taking shotguns and randomly killing relatives, fellow students, or teachers. But how many of these new cases they discovered are reactions to the medications they took to offset their problems? Often, the parents are in a quandary as to whether to follow the prescribed medical advice and hope for the best, or let it go. It's a *catch-22 situation*.

And then, in my mind, Jason's comments were written in ten-foot tall letters in *bold, bright flashing colors*. They are not humans, but things to work until their time is up, when they have outlived their usefulness, and are put away in another safe environment. I thought I was back in 1963, when my brother's problems began, of the breakdown a month before. Although I slept through most of it, I recalled that he made my parents nuts because he couldn't sleep or eat. He was totally stressed out. Why? My parents didn't know. There was nothing going on in our lifestyle that warranted this behavior. I don't remember whether Dad consulted his brother, a doctor, or took Bob to him. All I know is that he wound up in the hospital, and lost his friends because he was "tainted," for the use of a better term.

This area of Brooklyn was part of Bensonhurst, at that time associated with macho types. Many were tough, high school dropouts, and couldn't carry on a conversation without cursing. You had to fit an image and not wind up in a mental institution. There was great pride in strutting and flexing macho muscles up and down the highways and via the byways of Bensonhurst. Quite often, brains were cast aside, but were respected for those who lived in another neighborhood. A philosophy passed down from generation to generation, as far as I was concerned. How we ever wound up here and stayed with our constant quest for knowledge, education, and culture, I'll never know.

Ironically, none of his friends who dropped him as a friend fit the macho image. They were all college students like him, clean cut with many plans for the future once they graduated.

Today, this area has changed, and it has become quite ethnic with newly arrived immigrant families from Russia, Europe, Asia, or Central America. Worrying about mental problems is on the back burner. Instead, neighbors lend a hand in helping these families understand and adjust to their new neighborhoods, pointing out organizations that can help them and their children.

No matter how many medical experts are interviewed or programs are there to educate people on accepting people with physical or mental disabilities, the end results are the same. People with disabilities were labeled like they were in Nazi Germany—they have outlived their usefulness and were heard from no more. Of course, here, they were not eliminated—just ignored.

I was in a catatonic state. In 2001, I was more concerned, and I wondered if he would take a computer course or a cooking course—something to keep him occupied. I was livid, angry, and insulted. I questioned why this happened to him—why this happened to my parents.

In the 1990s, I was an associate producer, cohost, cameraperson, and guest on *Art for All; Arts for the Disabled*, a half-hour television program whereby each session was seen for a month at a time on WLIG, Cablevision, NY. For each segment, we interviewed, discussed, and showcased different groups of people in the arts—music, dance, drama—who are all dedicated to, produced for, part of or active in the arts for people with disabilities from all parts of the globe. How ironic, I thought, because I was interviewing people with disabilities who were now making great strides in their lives and the arts because of the changing attitudes of people towards the disabled and were being appreciated for overcoming their diversities. There were places for them to exhibit their artistic work or to perform theatrical talents. My God, has anything changed? What happened to my brother? What went wrong?

Memories of 302 Broadway

The Fordham Years

As usual, it must have been a beautiful end of summer day as it always was when school started. We knew we weren't going to the beach, but to school instead because we were embarking on another milestone in our lives—college. The 302 Broadway had three Fordham careers as majors—law, business, and education. We rarely touched base with business and law. Many colleges then admitted either men or women, but not both. By 1955, they were changing their enrollment requirements—women were being admitted to all-male colleges and vice versa, but not in all subjects. Fordham was one of them. The women were allowed to take courses in the education program. I chose to go to Fordham because my Uncle Frank, my dad's brother, went there before going to Georgetown Medical School. Also, there was always an aura of Fordham, I guess because of the reputation of their football team as well.

We followed like sheep into a classroom for orientation that was being conducted by Dr. Scanlon, (director of teacher training.) I was beside myself that day because I was attending coed school, thank heavens, and needed a real wardrobe, even better! For four years, I wore uniforms at Fontbonne Hall Academy High School. Now, I could wear what I wanted but still concerned whether or not what I was wearing was appropriate. I sat down, looked around, felt comfortable with the setting, and with me. I gave myself a passing grade. Hooray!

I hooked up with my high school friend, *Margaret and a soon-to-be new friend, *Merilee, and anxiously awaited the next step. I noticed that there were a lot of female students, and many of them were Italian-American. Then, I didn't know many women who had graduated in college, and, if any, were Italian-American. (Why I thought it mattered, I don't know, but then it did. I guess it was the familiar things about your own kind or safety in numbers.

Today, my crowd is diverse with the many interests, nationalities, and ages they represent.) There was a lot of excitement in the air as we were all freshmen ready to take on the world via four years in Fordham.

Yet, when I think back at my student participation at Fordham, I see that I was part of some clubs, but really, I attended class and went to work at Macy's, Gimbels, or A&S department stores as I didn't waste time and hang out. There was no campus—only City Hall Park, and it was not too enticing to sit there. I was involved as a freshman in one, big project that was important to all of us. One of our classmates, Arthur Street, was an ex-marine veteran (Korean War) who told us how lonely the soldiers were in the hospitals and needed cheering up. A group of us put together a USO show, which would go on tour in the veterans' hospitals. I was part of a line dance, *Black Bottom*. I went to one hospital in Staten Island, and two in New York. It was fun while it lasted. We couldn't figure out why so few soldiers smiled. When we found out that we were in the mental wards, I had to drop out as I was too upset about these men. Little did I know what my future held at that time.

Juggling student teaching, taking courses, and having a job or looking for a job after graduation was crazy, but we did it, and we all survived. Although the fashion industry was my first priority, teaching became a reality. The fashion industry took a backseat.

We had New York City at our command. We went to museums or Broadway shows and tried different restaurants whenever we could fit them into our schedules. Often, we walked to Chinatown and ate in many restaurants to try their specialties. When the Saint Gennaro Feast was on in Little Italy, we walked over to partake in and eat those delicious Italian delicacies that we knew were freshly made.

I had fun during those four years at Fordham. We were all agreeable and happy to help one another if need be. There was no viciousness or one trying to outdo another. When we student taught, we were only too happy to share our lessons or ideas with one another in our classes at 302. After all, we were not starry-eyed freshmen, but rather grown professionals ready to get out there and teach our craft.

In 1959, I graduated with a B.S. in Elementary Education from Fordham. In June, I had a job as a substitute teacher at PS 287K, and in September was hired to teach full-time. By March, a third of the staff was transferred to PS 46K on Clermont Avenue, a brand-new building not too far from where we were.

Now, it was time to focus on Bob's future.

Bob's Turn

Dad was willing to pay for day school for Bob, but Bob insisted on getting a full-time day job. The reason was obvious—girls. Dad gave us allowances but not big enough to take a girl out on a date. It was only a few dollars each week, hardly enough for a movie and a glass of water. Bob had bigger ideas than that for a date. The compromise position was that Bob could work if he took night classes. So, off he went to earn dollars during the day, and learn how to make more in a bachelor's program in Business Administration at night. And in between, Bob would look for girls on whom to bestow his largesse.

I've been told many times that Bob was a real charmer, and that the parents of almost every girl he dated treated him like royalty. Whenever I saw Bob with a girl (usually down the block), he would introduce me and gave me a smile that said, "Bye, bye." I took the hint. At home, I always asked him if she were his latest girlfriend. He just smiled and nodded, "Could be."

Perhaps the pressures that eventually overwhelmed Bob began to build at this time. Attending night school wasn't that easy for Bob. This was partly due to the fact that night students were considered second-class citizens then. And often, they were kept waiting for courses that closed out before they had a chance to register for them. Bob became increasingly frustrated with the process. Getting a good job for the day time was another problem.

Unfortunately, my brother did not have a job waiting for him when he graduated high school. He pounded the sidewalks, but it was impossible for him to find employment for two reasons. Firstly, when future employers noted that he was attending night school, they concluded that he would be likely to quit his job at any time to attend college full time. So Bob was caught in a catch-22, he didn't want to go to day school so he could get a job, but couldn't get a job because he went to night school. And to top it off, night school was becoming a never-ending story.

The second problem for Bob was that he was designated I-A in the draft. This meant that he was available for immediate service, if required. Many employers assumed he would be drafted and were unwilling to spend the time and effort training him just to lose him at a moment's notice. But prospective employers were not the only ones concerned with the possibility of Bob entering the service.

The thought of any future relative in the armed forces did not sit well with my family, especially my mother. Mom had three brothers who served in World War I and four nephews in World War II. Uncle Peter emerged unharmed; Uncle Paul was gassed and always had problems with his lungs until the day he died. The third, Uncle Joe, the youngest brother, was so gung ho to serve his country that he signed up three times, the first at fifteen years of age. My grandmother unvolunteered him twice! The third time, she let him follow his wishes and go to the front because the army wouldn't release him. Joe, the self-styled hero, was a true casualty of World War I. He was shell-shocked and missing in action for nine months. Within a short time of returning to the States, the pressure of daily life was too great for him to cope. Uncle Joe spent the rest of his life at the Northport V.A. Hospital in Long Island.

My family's luck was scarcely any better in World War II. Mom's three nephews, Raffi, Rocky, and John came back; the fourth, Richard, was killed in action on the shores of Tripoli, Italy during the week of his eighteenth birthday.

The frustrations for Bob continued to build as he tried to get past the twin logjams of a snail's crawl through night school and no luck on the job front. Finally, as my father suggested, Bob took the exams for civil service jobs. He passed the civil service exam and soon had a job at a desk. It may not have been much, but it was a white-collar job, and this meant progress. He seemed to be happy that his life was moving forward.

All seemed well until my brother turned twenty-three years old in 1963. Within a month's time, he changed. He dropped a lot of weight, which, with his thin built, made him look ghastly. He couldn't sleep, didn't shave, and he made my parents nuts by pacing up and down the house all night. My father called his brother, a doctor, who assured him that Bob was okay. However, Bobby's condition did not improve.

On January 25 of that year, the night before my mother's birthday, my brother became a full-time resident in the psychiatric ward of Pilgrim State Hospital in Deer Park, Long Island. My father put it a little more bluntly, "He's in the nuthouse."

The Shock, the Shame, the Pain

The first week after Bob was admitted to the hospital was surreal. My brother received a letter from the U.S. Selective Service Department ordering him to report to the local Army Recruitment Center. Mom was relieved by the silver lining to the cloud that Bob's illness presented—while she was unsure what exactly qualified someone as I-A, she did know for sure that someone in a mental hospital could not be qualified to serve in the military. I was not so sure that being in the army was so bad that an institution was counted as an improvement, partly because I did not have as direct an interaction with the casualties as my mother had had.

Just as we were coming to some terms with Bob's illness and reprieve from military service, one of Mom's older sisters, Aunt Mary, died suddenly from a heart attack. The world seemed to be crashing around our ears. By the end of the week, we shed all the tears our bodies allowed us to have. Grieved out, we returned to our daily lives and jobs in a daze.

Each evening, for weeks, Dad, Mom, and I sat across from each other in the living room in a state of shock and remorse. Those "kooks," "lunatics," those "lock them up forever" people we saw in the movies, on television, and the streets of whom we made fun, we now claimed as one of our own. All of a sudden, we had to look at ourselves and realize that we were wrong to immediately write off human beings that way. The problem was not with the lunatics, but with us. It was a lesson that we struggled to learn over and over again, as well as to teach to others. Little did I know, decades later, that I would still have to face the fact that the lesson had not been fully learned even by a close friend. But then again, I had a very long way to go myself at that point. My college education was no match for the images from the media of the time. Also, and perhaps even more importantly, there was the deep-seated fear to be different from others. But before we condemn the intolerance of those days (which did, of course, exist) we might ponder: is the current culture really as forgiving of differences, or does it merely have a new set of taboos?

I was a nervous wreck because I was a victim of those rumors about "those people," especially the type of students I taught. I never knew who was going to attack who, and when and if anyone was going to get hurt. Who was going to comfort me for my traumas?

Some nights, I would lie awake wondering over and over nonstop.

"What's going to happen when he comes home?" I pondered.

Weeks later, I finally mustered up the courage to mention what happened to my brother to my friends because, quite frankly, the words got stuck in my throat. Oddly, it was Merilee who seemed the most understanding. She stressed over and over that having mental problems was like having the measles. Truly, then, I was mortified and embarrassed. The stigma of having someone in your family in a mental institution was too much to bear, and I continued to try to keep it out of the limelight. Only now, years later, have I mustered the ability to share our family story.

Then, too, I compared the lives of my students with the life that I was living at home. Was there a difference or was it the same?

My mother and I went to the family priest to ask why this happened to *us*! I gave up on my uncle, the doctor, who also seemed to be in a state of shock as we were. No matter what I asked him, all I got from him was, "Could be…." I never knew whether he was protecting me or chose to discuss the situation with my parents instead. Was I that young that I couldn't fathom the seriousness of the problem? I was college-educated and a teacher myself! Yet I was still treated as a child.

"Sometimes things happen and we don't have the answers," the priest answered when I questioned him.

I looked him in earnest but simply replied, "Oh?" because I knew it was fruitless to continue the conversation any longer. I admit I never knew what conversations transpired between my father and uncle, or even my mother.

Once I went to see Bob with my father and uncle.

"Do you really know who I am?" asked my brother.

My brother, I hope. However, I blocked out the rest of that visit because I really couldn't handle him being that sick. I gave him a blank look because I never asked him to tell me what he meant by that comment. I told myself, *I didn't answer him because I didn't want to upset him then*. I told myself that maybe Bob was stressed out with issues that he couldn't discuss with anyone. But maybe it is closer to the truth that I was overwhelmed and afraid and did not want to know what he meant by that remark. I was so traumatized by the experience that I decided to wait until my brother would come home to ask him about that hint of a revelation. That was my resolution to myself, but I never did ask him.

My friends were very supportive, but I couldn't talk about this illness. Being educated did not change my attitude very much towards those who suffered from "that condition." My brother's sickness spoke louder than words.

I lived in the house with a person who was in a mental ward. I knew how they acted and reacted because my friends and I taught one problem child after another for four years now. Movies of the era with Dean Martin and Jerry Lewis did not hold people with mental problems as victims trapped in their bodies, but rather as pawns to be ridiculed. We used to talk about these characters and imitate their afflictions. For me, it was impossible to understand why Bob was there and why many of my students weren't. I cried in my pillow for weeks.

My mother did not travel. Every Sunday, she sent my dad to the hospital with Bob's favorite dishes that she personally prepared: spaghetti and meatballs, lasagna, manicotti, and veal parmigiana. She made anything her son wanted, including a thermos of freshly brewed coffee. My father didn't drive, so he did what many people did in the same situation. A black limousine pulled up every Sunday to take him and other parents or caring family members to Deer Park. They banded together for the long trek to visit their loved ones at Pilgrim State Hospital. Sometimes my uncle drove him to check my brother's progress.

But we would never discuss these visits, or Bob, directly, even though my father was a basket case after each visit. Everything was a secret, like the big "C" (cancer) in *Brighton Beach Memoirs*. I was not included in the conversation of my brother's condition when my father came home each week from the hospital. When Bob's condition was discussed, it was often in code and in broken fragments. I remember my Dad saying that it was possible that Bob's sickness was attributable to his breaking up with a girlfriend. Which one, I didn't know then nor now. However, Dad seemed vague in his statement and I never knew if that was his suggestion or the doctor's. Other times, he suggested that maybe it was combination of looking for a job for years.

When we needed to reassure ourselves, we would merely talk about how good and fresh he looked now. Most times the façade stayed in place.

One Sunday, I overheard my father tell my mother, "Bob looks good. He misses us." Then there was a pause before he added bitterly, "I don't understand how he wound up there." For the first time in my life, I heard my father sob aloud.

"Shhhhh. She'll hear you. Let's not upset her," Mom whispered, in true blue traditional style. "Let's not tell her, she'll be upset."

"Daddy and I will handle it. Have no fear. You just go to work," was the answer I received whenever I asked any questions.

And like a dutiful child, I did.

Grandma Nostro and Bob, 1941

Facing Friends, Neighbors, and Family

A few months later, Bob came home from Pilgrim State Hospital. He looked healthy and rested. The day he did come home, Bob walked through the front door, smiled, and we welcomed him with open arms. The stigma was gone. I could relax. Everything was back to normal. I could lift my head again. We were a normal family again.

Or so I thought.

Soon we began to rewrite the history of what had happened, sometimes with the help of the doctors. The psychiatrist told my dad that my brother had a physical breakdown and not a mental breakdown. I don't know whether my parents knew any more about this case or not because, as usual, that information was never passed down to me.

Explanations for Bob's breakdown were sought in anything that was external to the family. "You know, when Bobby was a kid, they thought he had meningitis." Years later, Dad turned to me after watching a program on causes of mental problems, stating, "Some of those people suffered from mental illness when they got older. Bobby's case was the tip of the iceberg."

How often I would hear him tell me this each time he saw a program on schizophrenia. Articles in *The New York Times* noted that some of these cases could be traced to a childhood illness, a virus. Then I made light of the comment until I read updated articles years after my father had passed away. Recently, I read that this was noted in the Merck Medical book. Who knows? Perhaps this was the secret to his illness. The doctors who took care of him are long gone, and, at the present time, I don't have access to his records.

Considering the breakthroughs and what we know about the mind now, these would reveal some truth, but mostly on the philosophies or trends towards dealing with mental illness, which were followed at that time. We even postulated that the problem may have come about because my brother was born at home, since my mother couldn't make it to the hospital in time.

Could it have been that the hospital would have caught and corrected whatever was wrong?

No.

But we needed the answer to be something outside ourselves and outside our control. We needed whatever had upset our vision of normal to be "out there." We needed there to be a fault, and we needed it to be with the faraway stars and not ourselves.

When some neighbors saw Bob, they practically walked around him, treating him like a leper. Most welcomed him home and gave words of encouragement to him and my parents. Sometimes they would nod to me and scoot back into the house as if it was a sin to say "hello" to me. You couldn't talk about it to anyone. It's *"old world* Italian" of dealing with serious issues. My parents weren't into that mentality. I guess it went along with the "evil eye" syndrome. Talk about it, and you'll catch it. Now, I understand that the neighbors felt it was improper to be nosy. They were savvy enough to realize that we had enough grief without having to dwell on it. Then, I didn't think that way. Instead, I was just hurt.

Unfortunately, Bob was soon completely isolated. His very well-educated friends were never home whenever he called them. There was always an excuse whenever they saw him and that they already made plans before he came. Bob did have one friend from the office who didn't strand him, or so we thought. My parents invited him over for dinner quite often. He ate well while he was our guest, but he never made plans to meet my brother in the city for a movie or dinner. I guess dinner at our house was enough friendship for him. My parents held their tongue because they were hurt. Bob, on the other hand, was happy that he had a day with a friend. Eventually, even my brother realized that he was being duped, and the "friend" was allowed to drift away. No one was at home for Bobby.

Poor Bobby, cured but convicted of being different, began to falter again. He asked my mother what he had done wrong. What could she do, but do as only a mother does best? She encouraged him to make new friends and cried silently when she was alone. Within a short time, Mom noticed the change in him. He was walking around during the night and not making sense. He wasn't taking the medication and making irrational comments. He was losing weight again. My mother was concerned about his job. Did they notice a change in him? Eventually, she made it clear to Dad and Uncle Frank that Bob was losing ground. Soon Bob was back in the hospital.

During the '60s, people mocked, rejected, and feared persons who had problems because they did not toe the line of being a normal human being. Originally, I thought that this attitude only applied to people who lived in this area. Over the past few years, I heard children then who were born with severe mental or physical disabilities, and were from *all nationalities*, whether in this neighborhood or others. Some, I might add, were never sent to school or let out of the house, or, worse still, were committed to an institution. The shame in their home was too great to share with outsiders. What a tragedy! Thank

God my parents were wise and savvy enough to have my brother join the real world again and not punish him by keeping him out of the public eye. As I write this, I realized it's a good thing for me, or I would have been up a creek! Guess it was not the time to have any obvious mental or physical problems.

Months later, when Bob was discharged again, the doctors told Dad that he would be able to hold a stress-free job, but not on the executive level. At school, I consulted fellow teachers and guidance counselors as to whether this was such a good option.

They said, "Of course. Not everyone recoups to hold down a full-time job!"

My parents were delighted with the good news, and said, "Who cares?" Bob had a job with the NYC _____. His job description, "clerk," also meant "mailroom." And he worked in that position until he retired. Bob went from being a cute guy to a cute guy with *special needs*. This affliction, since he was never cured, included monthly visits to the therapist and every three months to the psychiatrist, plus a nightly dose of two milligrams of Haldol or the like from the New York Mental Health Center. We felt confident that Bob was in good hands because the medical profession knew more than we did, and we trusted their expertise. Whatever medication was prescribed, they informed my parents to contact them immediately if they noted any side effects of the drugs. They did, and a new medication was given to him. Most importantly, he had someone to confide and trust in should problems requiring professional guidance arose.

New Career

When Bob returned to work at his new workstation, his desk job was a thing of the past. One day, when our schedules were back to normal, I sat back and went over the scenario. Things were really not the same. When my friends visited us, he came downstairs to greet them. They *hello*ed back with big, wide, frozen grins on their faces and fear etched in their eyes. Bob walked over to them, but they edged their way to the other side of the sofa, away from him, women as well as men.

I didn't say anything because I couldn't. We were all taught in the same area or schools, and we all had the same attitude towards mental patients. I prayed for the floor to swallow us from view. But that didn't happen.

Why am I doing this to him and myself? I thought. It broke my heart but, hey, I swallowed my pride, put on a happy face, and faced the music.

I found myself surrounded by stories of ordinary people—all nationalities, folks like us—who have had several breakdowns, severe ones with shock treatments, and those who bounced back to reality. There was hope! But then again, they weren't Italian-American instilled with lifetime of superstitions about the demons, evil eyes, or whatever else could possibly befall you. Ironically, my parents were never into "the evil eye" *malocchio* or other superstitions. I asked my parents how come they didn't believe in these superstitions. And they just looked at me and rolled their eyes.

"Oh, please, grow up! Is that why we sacrificed ourselves to send you to Fontbonne Hall and Fordham? Ask the nuns and priests what they think of these superstitions!" was Mother's response.

As time went on, I bounced back to my life, and continued traveling, skiing, dating, and pursuing life. My parents were in charge of my brother; I was outta there. They became his friends and confidants. Mom made sure he was dressed properly and even tied his shoelaces. To her, everyone was watching him to see if there were any defects. If he did, it was a reflection on her on how she brought him up. Her attitude, too, was that looking good helped to build a healthier self.

Dad and Uncle Frank would take Bob on vacations every year from fishing in New England to touring Nova Scotia, Montreal, Washington, D.C., or Williamsburg, Virginia. My brother seemed to enjoy himself, but Dad complained that Bob would leave early in the morning for breakfast on his own. For dinner, he would order the biggest lobster on the menu. I asked my brother on his reaction to Dad's complaint.

"When you're with two older people or gentlemen, namely, Uncle Frank and Dad, you gotta do what you gotta do to enjoy oneself," Bob answered with a smile and continued. "These two guys think I'm two years old. I like to go for a walk, have a nice meal by myself, and buy newspapers from the towns we're visiting to see what's going on in these places. How else do you learn about the people? They don't have headlines like New York papers, but they tell stories about the people in their town. I guess they watch television for the real news."

I thought about what he said. No matter where I traveled to, Bob would ask me to bring him a newspaper from that place. There were no requests for special sweaters or liqueurs; just newspapers. He got a kick of what news items the newspapers thought important to print. His hobby continued even as we traveled from place to place. He had more choices because he could buy up all the newspapers from that particular town we visited.

Transitions

In 1978, I made a huge decision on my life. I went back to school to fulfill my long-time desires to be a costume designer, playwright, and writer. My parents' reaction to this was very different than their attitude towards college. Back then, Mom said emphatically, with trumpets of righteousness sounding behind her, "We don't support starving artists. You will have a real job at the end of four years. You will become a teacher. The children need you. You'll never make it as a secretary because you hate typing. Forget being a nurse because you have no patience. The patients will jump out of the window."

As I think back, I figured out that my mother complained I had too much energy when I was young, and I made her nuts because I couldn't sit still, so she said I should volunteer my time to help others. Volunteering was known as "payback time," because I was so lucky that the universe (whether that was specifically God or Mom was a theological territory I dared not tread) required that I give something back to the community. Mom had a lot of Jewish friends who told her that when you are lucky, you pay back to help others. In those days, being lucky was having two doting parents, a roof over my head, and food on the table. If I dared question her decision, she would give lectures on how many families did not have these advantages, even in the very neighborhood in which we lived. Naturally, Marie, my next door childhood friend, and I, volunteered our time at Saint Finbar's Church because her mother agreed with mine and was not going to concede that her family was any less fortunate than ours.

Father Donegan was only too glad to see two more volunteers. At thirteen, we taught catechism (called CCD, today) to elementary school kids on Sunday, and became part of the Legion of Mary Society for ladies. I joined the choir and played basketball as well. Father said I was a good leader or a responsible person and did a good job. From that remark, Mom concluded, ergo, that I would also make a good educator.

Years later, when I taught in the NYC school system, I always wanted to live in the city on the East Side where many of my friends now lived. When I transferred out of PS 46k in 1968, it never worked out because the school I applied to in the East 50s only needed one teacher. The principal already had the one person. The second choice was in Staten Island, a beautiful new grammar school. When I drove there and saw how barren it was, all I could think of was that I'd never see this place when it snows. My third choice was Shell Bank Junior High (I.S. 14K). I was so anxious to transfer out that I didn't realize it was a junior high.

The principal, Mr. Solomon, asked me to check with the Board of Education on whether I could stay with my K to 6 license. They okayed it. A short time later, a new friend of mine, Brenda, from this staff rented an apartment on E. Fifty-Fifth Street, between First and Second Avenue, in a new building. Great! I'll rent an apartment there, too. But then she complained that it took too long to get to Brooklyn in the morning, and at 3:00 P.M. stayed at her mother's until the parking rules went off. I lived twenty minutes from work. I stayed home.

It's always easy to get married, have kids, and concern yourself as my friends did with marriage issues, kids, problems, and the rest of the *magilla*. I wanted my life to take a more creative path. Once I started doing costumes for the shows with our one-dollar budget per costume (exaggerated, of course, thanks to the generosity of the NYC Board of Education for art funds) in the After School Center at Shell Bank Junior High, and I was also designing Off-Off-Broadway for TRG and starred in their production of *Little Murders* (Jules Feiffer), I more than realized that this was for me—except for the acting part. I never acted in my life, and it takes a special kind of guts to go up in front of people and perform. In this play, all I had to do was to knit scarves during the wedding scene in someone's house. I sat on the couch and knitted away. I had no dialogue. My hands shook because I was so nervous.

Friends who came were hysterically laughing because they noticed my hands shaking. They appreciated the scarves, though, that I made as Christmas gifts. The gift card read, "From the play, *Little Murders.*" My friend, Danny Clancy, a devoted attendee of the junior high plays I worked on, and who became my mentor, said: "Why don't you take one course in the Program for Educational Theater at NYU? I know you. You'll never leave." Truer words were never spoken.

I took his advice. In 1978, when I sat in Nellie McCaslin's "Children Theater," I knew this was where I wanted to be. I finished a master's in two years and "teched," or designed, lots of NYU productions. It paid off. In 1980, I was hired as a fellow costume designer for the doctorate program.

What makes costume designing so intriguing is that you never know when an idea for a design will pop up from something you have seen in the past—like a color from a bouquet of flowers, a painting, or a fabric pattern. It's mind-boggling. I kid you not!

When fellow classmates set up their own theater companies, I became their costume designer. Eventually, one by one, they gave up the company. As I look back, I think it was because, as much as we did a lot of good theater based on the critics' reviews, we outgrew each other, and needed to move on to the next step of our careers.

I know that Mom cried when she found out I was costume designing. She had to quit school after the eighth grade and become a seamstress to help support her family. I didn't. She would have been a very good lawyer because we argued about court cases constantly. She only saw me as a teacher. I explained to her, loud and clear, that I will always be a teacher! Enough already! I reminded her that it was her fault and Aunt Jenny's as well. She was an interior decorator and always at our house. I grew up listening to them talking about and comparing styles and fabrics of clothes and decorating. So what did she expect? Maybe Mom knew more than me as to what my aim in life was to be.

I soon finished a master's in educational theater at NYU and was now working on a doctorate in the same field. I had been hired as a costume designer/teaching fellow (I designed and was a "technie;" no teaching was required) for the program from 1980-83, and then finished the course work. I fancied myself as part of the faculty of a New England university.

One thing I learned from teaching was turning a negative into a positive, and being a returning student in the MA and Ph.D. program, I found I was using this philosophy more and more. I wanted to be a playwright. It was time to work in a more professional setting other than a university school setting. In September 1985, I enrolled in a playwriting class taught by Brother Jonathan, O. S. F., at the Ensemble Studio Theater on the West Side in New York City. Things were going well, and I felt the creativity in me starting to bloom.

Then, that November, my mother died suddenly.

"When I get ready to die, then I'll go to the hospital."

And she did! She was dead in less than two weeks from extreme hardening of the arteries. I was now a single parent to my father and brother.

The night my Mom died, I sat on my bed and started writing a scene about two friends—one who was going through marital strife, and the other, me, footloose and fancy free becoming Mrs. Mom, a parent to an aging father and his son—in a play I aptly called *Transitions*.

Working on a doctorate, designing costumes, being a playwright, and teaching elsewhere took a backseat. Now, I *had* to stay in New York City. Dad was eighty-four. How could I leave? Bob, bless his soul, was a caring son but could not conceive of himself as Mr. Mom nor was he really up for the job. But all was not lost.

I was designing *Fiddler on the Roof* at a community theater for a friend whom I used to teach with. He was glad I didn't drop out because of Mom's passing. I assured him that since I wasn't leaving New York, I would continue working on the show. Besides, what more could I ask for? It was so convenient—fifteen minutes from my house.

At the end of the term in February, we each had our moment of fame, and *Transitions* was presented as part of Brother Jonathan's One-Act Festival. Although everyone encouraged me to finish the play, I assured them that *Transitions* was a one-act play. Audiences loved it and identified with it. Now, my playwriting career was going slowly because I wasn't sure how much free time I would have to follow my dreams.

The main focus of my life was teaching English in a junior high, as I hadn't retired yet, and parenting my elders. Who knew? Who would have thought this was my "new future?"

What about Bob? How did he fit into this picture? He did show up at the hospital and funeral home for Mom. A rarity because, in the past, he refused or just stuck his nose in to view the body and leave. Everyone was understanding and forgave him for his actions. Now, I had to assure him what my aim was to be for his future.

"Stop worrying. I am not going to desert a sinking ship. You won't have to cook or clean. I'm going to be here forever and a day," I reassured him when he looked sad because he knew I wanted to teach elsewhere.

"Good girl," he responded with a smile. "That takes a load off my mind."

But parenting now for the two of them? Oh, my God!

The New Me—Chief,
Cook, and Bottle Washer

I had always regarded my father as very Americanized since he attended Cooper Union College and seemed to have escaped the typical Italian male route of his day by not having a blue-collar job. I think it's safe to say that my brother and I were probably the only kids on the block whose father was a college graduate. Our neighbors were quite respectful to us because of Dad's degree in higher education. Many wished that their children would go to college and succeed as he did. Dad changed when Mom died.

Although Dad was eighty-four, he was still *our* young daddy. He was still doing our income taxes and chipping the base of the Christmas tree to insert in the iron stand, a family relic, every year. Everything was fine, that is, until I cooked.

During the first dinner together, Dad gave his worldly words of wisdom.

"Your mother meant well, but she babied you. You've got to be more independent. Get your own checking account."

That didn't come until after Dad died because it was easier to just have Dad and me on the joint checking account. To my brother, he offered these kind words, "I'm giving you some sound advice. Count on this one," he said in mock humor, "for dinner. Don't ask her for breakfast or lunch." He put his fingers on his lips warningly. "This one is not like the other one. She was good; this one's a bitch! Besides, we don't know if she really can cook!"

My brother laughed and so did I, because it was so funny. I cooked since I was thirteen years old. However, Coquilles Saint Jacques were more my speed than pasta, lasagna, and the like. Quite frankly, I wasn't interested in cooking, since I ate out most of the time. Also, who could compete with Mom's cooking? It was her domain.

Mom, despite her endearing qualities, possessed an annoying habit—she could never give me any credit for knowing how to cook. "What does she know about cooking? She's single!"

She sounded as though she thought a wedding ring served double duty as a decoder ring for how to master marinara sauce. No matter how many times I chewed her out for these comments, she waved me off. However, in my heart, I'm convinced that she was jealous of my fondness for and expertise in French cooking.

With Dad, it was another story.

The first time I made broiled chicken, Dad raised his cane and raised Cain about how much money he had spent on food. He then left the dining room and stormed (to the extent an octogenarian *can* storm) into the living room to watch TV. I screamed back, "Hey! I don't care! That's fine with me!" I looked at my brother and said, "What the hell is his problem?"

"Mom always took the skin off," Bob laughed and answered in a matter-of-fact tone.

"Christ," I answered him, "do I need this abuse for a three- inch piece of skin?"

Bob shrugged and left the table to join Dad in the living room.

At other times, I left broiled, marinated spare ribs, with corn on the cob, salad, and ice cream for dessert. Rather a safe and hearty meal, with no complaints for a change, or so I thought. My friends called while I was out. My father complained in *an-ever-so-quivering voice*, that *he paid good money* for the food, and, I, the ingrate, left him *bones, bones*. Needless to say, my phone rang off the hook, bright and early the next morning.

"How could you do that to your father? Leaving him bones?" My friends wanted to know.

"He's got to be kidding, right?" I told Bob what happened.

"They were too skinny for ribs," Bob answered philosophically.

From then on, I relied on my brother to fill me in on tidbits about Dad and continued making the traditional pasta dishes. I guess I didn't expect to stay at this parenting party too long. The faster the adjustment, the easier it was on my nerves. My brother handled the bank jobs—to take out or deposit whatever Dad requested. I handled the rest of the household, construction, and paint jobs. Since I got home at 3:30 P.M., it was easier for me to do many of the chores. We worked well together as a team. Whatever fights we had were usually between Dad and me over his brand of humor, my cooking, and my attitude. My brother was off the hook because he worked longer hours than I did.

I couldn't leave Brooklyn for an out-of-state job, but I could travel. Whenever I did, I learned my lesson to say the least and cooked whatever Dad liked, label it, and froze in the freezer. I even listed what time the frozen dishes should be defrosted and heated up. I gave a copy of the menus to my cousin, Palma, who was my mother's confident and now mine. There was an eight-year difference in their ages, but she was more than twenty years older than me. She was also my godmother.

"Go to Bay Ridge," Mom said when was dying, which meant adopting Palma as "our mother."

Palma was terrific because she called every morning and afternoon to double-check on what had to be done. Thank God, too, for the wonderful invention of the microwave. The last thing I needed was to call home and hear a complaint, such as the tomato sauce being too cold or the food is not defrosted enough and that they had to eat it *that* way! Bob was also in charge while I was gone. Each day, he called Dad to make sure he followed the directions as well. What was in a few telephone calls to Dad each day? Besides, Bob rarely took a vacation day and always went to work instead. In reality, he didn't like traveling anymore. Of course, I did, felt guilty, and was depressed because my life changed so much and wasn't ecstatic about my new "parenting demands."

In the past, with the exception of Christmas and New Year, I was always gone for the holidays. Usually, I skied up at Stowe or Sugarbush, Vermont or sunned myself on some beautiful tropical island like Puerto Rico, Antigua, or Bermuda. I belonged to the Sunrise Ski Club, and we managed to get reasonable group rates whenever we went up as a group. In the summer, I traveled for a month or two to Europe or attended conferences on costume design or educational theater. I always managed to get good rates for hotels and tours. I always had enough money to travel. If I didn't, I worked in the after-school centers, designed shows, took out loans, and kept a very good eye out for good travel bargains. I always got good rates when I attended conferences, since there were discounts at many of the hotels.

Now, for every holiday, I stayed home and cooked up a storm, just like my mother had done. Although I knew I could go away for a month or two, I felt guilty leaving Dad alone in the house for hours until Bob came home. Even though he had the TV, his CDs, and a pipe, there were no friends or relatives closely by to sit with him. All his close confidants were long gone. I had my pre-Christmas parties again as before because it gave me a chance to decorate, be creative, and see friends I hadn't seen all year.

As the newest member of the Susie Homemaker Club, a group I adamantly refused to acknowledge for years, I planned some interesting meals. Basically, I stuck to the traditional dishes that my mother cooked, or purchased an unusual pâté for the holidays from Balducci's wonderful gourmet establishment in the city or a new liqueur from the nearest liquor store. Dad was either impressed or he just gave up and stopped nagging me about my cooking. Inviting friends for dinner cheered me up, as well as my "responsibilities." Pleasant conversation and jokes abound throughout the evening. Dad, Bob, and I also ventured to eat in new restaurants that lifted all our spirits.

My father, of course, let nothing pass him by. I was off the hook temporarily about my cooking, but Bob was another story.

"When did you eat last? Christ! Come up for air."

He hated to see Bob chomping down his food. When you're home, certain behavior patterns are acceptable. Out of the home, they were not. My father simply said in a low voice, "*Sporcaccione!* Slob! Did I need this aggravation?"

I was appalled, too, when my brother picked up the veal cutlet with his hand because he was too lazy to cut it with a knife. Was it that he forgot he was not at home, or did he not remember how to eat in decent restaurants in New York? When we had company, I warned him not to pick the food up with his hands because it was rude and disgusting. Life improved. Bob listened and did the right thing.

Since neither my brother nor I were married, we did have to hear occasionally about the lack of grandchildren making a ruckus or racing through the house. We convinced Dad that he was more important and could have our undivided attention.

"Wasn't that more important?"

"Sure," he agreed.

End of conversation.

And So...My New Lifestyle Continues

Once the food situation was under control, the next step of my parenting technique for the two men was to change their wardrobe. I dragged my father and brother to Rothman's Men's Department Store on Seventeenth Street and Park Avenue, it listed as Park Avenue South in the city, for new winter coats, raincoats, and sport jackets.

"Why do I need clothes? Where do I go? I'm an old man who sits on the porch and smokes my pipe," Dad moaned and groaned all the way to Manhattan. That changed when he stood in front of the mirror, pleased by what he saw. Also, my brother, in the past, tormented my mother whenever they went shopping. Most of the time, he left her chatting away, unbeknown to her, in an empty space vacated by him because of the way she spoke to him. Mother meant well, but patronizing my brother in public was not the wisest of all things. Now, it was my turn to deal with Bobby.

"You need a raincoat, an overcoat, and a sport jacket. Try these on."

I started my routine with a simple and direct statement (also known as the teacher's voice) as I counted the minutes I had left with these two distinctive personalities. He grunted and mumbled just like Dad but agreed. After he put the coat on, I led Bob to the full-length mirror, with the salesman smoothing the shoulders and fixing the lapels, adjusting the shoulders and patting him on the back with a final, "Good fit. No alterations needed either."

I was startled. For a minute, I thought he said altercation (so much for the importance of a letter of the alphabet). Bob smiled without any comments.

"Of course, you're happy," Dad remarked to Bob in his usual skeptical style and added, "everything we bought is the top of the line. Remember, your sister said that they're the gifts for Christmas and our birthdays. We owe her nothing. It's for free."

"Dad, give us a break. If Rosalie wants to be a good Santa, so what?" Bob answered. My brother didn't have to say anything. I knew by the tone of his voice that he was content. At times, he was a man of a few words.

When the salesman adjusted the clothes as he tried them on, he looked at himself in the mirror more than once. He was happy, too, by the attention he was getting. I knew by the tone of his voice that he was happy for the choices.

"My wonderful son spoke out. What else can I say?"

Everything we wanted was measured, altered if needed, paid for, and was to be sent by UPS, or, since I was the designated driver, I was also the designated pick upper of the newly, purchased treasures. We went home in peace.

Dad—Keeping Him Occupied and Interested in Life

At eighty-five years of age, Dad made an important decision in his life. He refused to do our income taxes because he wanted to spend the rest of his life "as an old man." That was it! No matter how much we protested, he refused to back down. No matter how many times we called him our "Young Daddy," he shook his head and refused to back down. I did them instead, and Dad was hit with five or six thousand dollars in back taxes. I called an accountant who informed me that Dad didn't claim his Social Security benefits. When I confronted him, he stated:

"I get this *little* check every month, my pension check, and that's it."

"Where's the other *little* check?" I asked.

"Never heard of it; you're mistaken."

I went through his papers. I found that he had "Direct Deposit," and asked Bob if he knew that Dad had "Direct Deposit."

"He tells me to take money out or to put it in. Never checked to see anything else because he never asked me to."

How irritated was I? Very irritated. I was even more irritated because I could not argue with Bob's reasoning. Now, I had another job—keeping tabs on out accounts for the IRS.

At eighty-eight years old, my dad was getting forgetful. A neighbor found him wandering outside in the rain because he was, "Going to work on Franklin Street."

This was a serious problem because that was the tenement where he lived in the 1920s. Those tenement buildings were long gone, as they are all part of New York City government buildings. I hired Eleanor, a friend of the family to care for Dad, a daddy sitter, until I came home from school. Originally, he resisted when he found out she was single.

"Let's her find a husband," he snapped.

I informed him that either she comes to work for us or off he goes to an old man's home with old nurses and no blonde ones to take care of him. After the first day, Dad said he was so happy with Eleanor that he would not want to die because she was a good and caring woman.

Eight years before, Dad gave up reading novels and *The Times* because he was afraid that he would die before he finished them. He felt they were too long, and sometimes too boring. Give him, *WINS, WINS New York,* on the radio or listen to his opera while he smoked a pipe. I bought the latest videos on Pavarotti or other opera notables. He kept an eye out for the PBS specials on operas or ballets. I remember walking into the house and hearing, "The Nutcracker Suite" blasting on the stereo, and him watching the football game on TV, and, of course, smoking his pipe.

This was enough entertainment for him. Each morning, Bob and I would put *The New York Daily News* in front of him to get him to read the headlines to keep him fresh and alert.

"Why do I have to read anything more than a paragraph?" he mumbled.

"That's ridiculous," I argued, "keep reading, our little young Daddy."

When Bob came home from work, he and Dad would discuss baseball or football games, arguing the difference between the capable players or the better teams.

With all the craziness of running a household, caring for two grown-ups, and teaching junior high English, I still managed to design two more musicals, *Mame* and *Annie* for my friend, Steven. By 1989, I finished *Transitions*. It was now a full-length play. Bob was now included as the brother who couldn't understand why his friends deserted him after he had a breakdown years earlier. My friend, Marvin Kahan, directed a staged reading at TRG, his Off-Off Broadway theater company. Most of the friends who showed up were shocked because they knew I designed plays, not write them. At the same time, I was still writing my dissertation on Broadway costume designer Patricia Zipprodt (*Pippin, Sunday in the Park with George, Fiddler, 1776,* and *Don Juan*), or at least I was trying to do so. I was too distracted and no gimmick could get me to focus on the project.

In December of that year, my father went to his HMO Medical Center and was told that he had a cold; a simple cold. In reality, it was pneumonia. God knows how long he had pneumonia because from then on, Dad never felt well. He didn't rally as he had before when he had a cold. It took Dad forever to walk down the steps in our house, let alone the outside steps. By mid-January, when he didn't improve, I was concerned and decided to take him back to the doctor. We were steady visitors. Whatever test was needed, Dad took it. Nothing seemed to help. Fortunately, he fell on my foot as I tried to get him into the car. A passerby helped put him into the car. I took him immediately to Victory Memorial Hospital, only to find out that he had pneumonia, a bleeding ulcer, a fever, and then some.

The doctor admonished me and demanded to know what kind of a daughter was I that I didn't take him for medical help sooner. I sat there stunned. Here I was, happy that he was getting real help. To top it off, I was up twenty-four hours straight waiting for a room, and now I had to deal with these accusations! This was the beginning of the long descent and decline of my father's health, going back and forth like a shuttle service, from the hospital bed in Victory Memorial Hospital back to the hospital bed in the living room, the latter being our makeshift hospital ward.

I was fortunate in having the most wonderful caring aides from all parts of the globe, namely, India, Guyana, and Haiti. I thought I was lucky, until one night, my brother walked in with a loaf of white Silvercup bread and announced in a loud and clear voice: "This is American bread. I bought it with American money. If you are American, you may have some."

I almost died because we were brought up never to be prejudiced. I thought my brother was flipping out and couldn't understand it, since I knew that most of the people he worked with were minorities. Oh, no, not him, too! What the hell was he saying? Living with a terminally ill patient is traumatic enough without having to worry about a second as well. In the midst of my father's illness, I realized that I had neglected Bobby. All I needed was for him to break down again. I called my godmother, Palma, once again—my backup person when instant help was needed. I whispered to her what happened. She asked to speak to him, and I ran out of the house on the pretense of seeing a friend.

"But what did I say? I didn't do anything wrong. What was so terrible about that?"

I heard hear her screaming at him and him protesting. As I think back, this was the only incident that shook me up regarding my brother at the time.

Bob accepted his share of the responsibility of caring for Dad more than I thought he would. For the rest of this long drawn out nightmare, he spent hours trying to cheer my father up with sports—baseball and football games, opera albums, or listening to Frank Sinatra on the radio on Saturday nights.

When Dad was brought back to the hospital, the responsibilities became more intense. I kept the round-the-clock aides in the hospital as well. I took no chances because I wanted them at his beck and call. The hospital was five minutes from the house by car, and I drove there very easily every afternoon or evening. Unfortunately, it was thirty minutes by bus from the R train in Bay Ridge.

Bob insisted on visiting Dad after work every night. His hours were 10:00 A.M. to 6:00 P.M., and he worked in Manhattan by City Hall. He got off at the Eighty-Sixth Street station and Fourth Avenue, took the bus to Eighty-Sixth Street and Seventh Avenue, and walked six blocks or waited for another bus. It was rather late by the time Bob reached the hospital, and so he stayed only ten minutes, and then headed home because he was hungry and beat.

I realized that it was the stress of the situation that was beginning to get to him. I suggested that if he had any problems, he should see his therapist or psychiatrist since he was still an outpatient of the NYC Mental Health Center; he did. Yes, that was one of the continuing perks of being discharged from a state institution. I called her myself with an update of Dad's health and how Bob was coping with the stress. I also made a deal with him to visit Dad two nights and skip the third. On the weekends, he would go in the daytime, and, since I drive, I visited Dad in the nighttime. We wanted to show that someone was always there to be with him. Anyone who had to care for a person twenty-four hours a day or set up with that kind of schedule knows what I mean.

Fortunately, my school workload made it easier to visit my father. Since I had been working at Shell Bank Junior High School in Sheepshead Bay since 1968, and because the hospital was close by, I was able to visit Dad whenever I had a long enough break during the day, without having to worry whether or not I would get in trouble, which was a blessing.

First, the pneumonia cleared up, then it was emphysema, and on and on, one new problem after another, as his body was breaking down or shutting down. At one point, the doctors thought he had a tumor in his lungs. Thank God, the X-rays were negative. Thank God for small favors. When Dad came home the first time, he turned to me and said, "Saw my mother. She said, 'not yet.'"

I was a basket case and realized that, as hard as it was, I had to snap out of it; otherwise, my brother would be grieving for the two of us. Confiding to anyone was no help because when you're pushed against the wall by fate, there is no answer. Dad's body was breaking down. It was the natural course of nature at his advanced age. The stress was getting to me, so I went to the principal and suggested that I quit before the situation started impairing my ability to teach and perform my other duties at school.

"What are going to do at home? Cry? You're not helping yourself or the situation. You need to stay healthy and focused. You're dealing with a full plate," said Dr. Friedman, principal, and also Jack Kaufman, assistant principal. Realizing that there was a therapeutic aspect to the work, as well as feeling a sense of responsibility to my students and colleagues, I stayed on and was mindful that life sometimes requires us to bear things we would never have imagined we could possibly bear.

Bob also displayed a strength of which I would never have dreamed him capable. I was proud of my brother since he handled his responsibilities well. In the past, he never visited anyone besides my mother in the hospital. I gave him the latest medical news, stopping only when it was clear he was too distressed to hear more. I realize that both of us were addicted to the hope that Dad would pull through. Of course, deep down there was the reality that this was the end for my dad. I chose to walk around my room at night while my brother slept soundly.

In October 1990, we took Dad home to spend his last days with us because we all wanted it that way. When he died, Bob and I sat across from each other, not saying a word for hours. The adjustment of both of us together presented us with a challenge of who was going to win. There was no way he was going to be coddled as in the past. He had to share in more decision-making about running a household.

A few months later, I retired from the Board of Education. Lucky that I waited as I wanted to retire a year earlier, but was encouraged to stay. The Board offered a buyout to those who had served thirty years and were under fifty-five years of age, and added a three-year bonus. However, being Mrs. Mom to only one person instead of two did not cut the work in half. After so many years teaching in school, all of a sudden, even simple arithmetic betrayed me!

Bob and me, Spring Lake, NJ. 1996, photo by Marie Pionegro

New Adjustments

B ob and I opened a joint checking account to pay for the house bills and whatever Bob needed. He learned how to sign checks, as he didn't believe in charge accounts. Would you believe this guy? Bob was given a chance for input whenever decisions had to be made regarding the upkeep of the house. With me in the lead, his suggestions were merely suggestions, since spending money was not one of his favorite pursuits.

He learned that when his bank CD was due, it was his responsibility to find out the best rate for six months, nine months, or a year, all simple everyday things we took for granted. The idea of a brokerage account or anything fancier than a CD was not even an option. But even a certificate of deposit wasn't easy because he was very mistrustful. When work was done for the house, I casually told him what his share was to be. He opted to pay for the cleaning lady and the delivery of *The New York Daily News*—less than a hundred dollars a week. Not too much to add to the coffers of a household, but it was better than nothing. At that point, I was happy that he could now relax in a stress-free atmosphere.

Thank God, the mortgage was long paid off! I recalled that my parents were originally going to leave the house to him only because they knew I was always looking to relocate. The issue resolved itself without anyone having to give it a thought. I said that I would stay in New York. Things have a funny way of working themselves out, though I have to admit, I do not always share life's sense of humor.

My brother had always slept in the smallest bedroom and never complained. Now, I willed him the master bedroom for several reasons. I hated sleeping in the back of the house because no matter who lived there, a dog barked all night. Maybe the dog owned the place and rented it out. Bob didn't hear it, so the dog didn't bother him. Lastly, I wanted his bedroom for an office. I was still working on a dissertation and needed that room to write. Ultimately, I still wanted to be a writer and playwright.

I worried about whether Bob's dreams were being fulfilled. He replied to one attempt to sound him out, "I'm okay. I like living in my house. I like living on this block. I like living in Brooklyn. I like working in the big city. Stop being so nosy!"

Friends and family warned me not to be upset if he refused to sleep in my parents' bedroom. Were they kidding? Bob was almost six feet tall! Who would turn down a new carpet, lamps, bedspread, drapes, ceiling fan fixture, and freshly painted walls? He had his own phone line, a new television, a lounge chair, and a growing wardrobe in which he picked and chose whatever he wanted to wear for work. More importantly, he had plenty of room to stretch his long legs. He certainly didn't resist this change!

There were times when I questioned whether or not I was ready for this latest challenge. I knew I wasn't just his sister. I was the chief, cook, and bottle washer. With Dad, Bob and I worked hand-in-hand to make our father comfortable. We could pretend we were both little kids and refer to our father as "our little Daddy." This was different. I knew I was going to be giving up more of my time and dreams until we adjusted to the new situation. I was pretty optimistic overall since I felt that after dealing with a hundred fifty junior high school personalities, one working man would be a snap.

Am I Ready?

S ocially speaking, my brother had no life outside of work. After putting in his hours in the mailroom, he either came home or stopped in J&R's near City Hall for CDs. At first, the only albums he would buy were Elvis's. Shelves groaned under the weight of the King of Rock and Roll. Eventually, his tastes broadened (perhaps because he already owned everything that Elvis had released) and added Pink Floyd, Frank Sinatra, Cream, Dave Matthews, Motown, the Rolling Stones, and the Beatles. He didn't like musicals or operas. When I played one of my albums, he would just sit there complacently until they were over because he knew it was useless to argue with me about what he thought about "those silly songs."

Bob was funny about money. He appreciated the CDs, especially if they were gifts, which meant someone cared, and they didn't cost him anything. It was at this time when I nicknamed him "My Twenty-Dollar Man" because no matter what the cost was, especially if it cost more than twenty dollars, he would only give me that amount. In his mind, this is what he calculated the costs should be. He never elaborated on his twenty-dollar decision, but I knew it included clothes and restaurants as well. As he said, the bills didn't like to leave his wallet. When we went out and he took out the twenty-dollar bill, my friends and I would laugh. Bob was a living Jack Benny.

"This all I can afford," he would say. He would refuse to pay the full price for a meal, explaining, "I think that is all this dinner is worth." For him, obviously, the right-hand side of the menu was only a suggestion.

However, there were nights when Bob sat in the kitchen with his head down, not talking. I wondered what he thought about. When I asked him, he just shrugged his shoulders and never shared those thoughts with me. When I discovered he loved old movies like I did, I ordered the total Cablevision package, which was very therapeutic for him. With this addition to our household, whenever we had company, we discussed and compared new and old movie themes and stories. Whoever called Bob mentioned the movie he/she saw, and they would discuss the film as if they were critics. Yet, I wondered why he cried like me when we watched these movies. Was it because it reminded him of the past and how our lives were different then? My brother developed a love for Hollywood gossip via "Access Hollywood" or "Page 6" of the *New York Post* and the like. He spent many nights chatting with friends about the "in" people.

Of course, I never knew whether Bob would be cured. My mother and father both swore that when they died, he would be cured. Perhaps if they babied him less and let him grow up more, he would have. Did he improve? Yes, but there were always those personal demons that he saw or heard. I didn't know. He wouldn't tell me. I knew when they were around because he would mention snakes, or what looks like a snake.

"You're imagining things. I never mentioned any snakes."

The only time I heard him speak about them was when the doctor in the St Vincent's Hospital in Staten Island asked him if he saw them. Bob answered "yes." Years later, I read in an article that some people who have schizophrenia call out and see, "snakes." I guess it's the nature of the illness.

Yet, he discussed any topic and held his own in the news, politics, entertainment, or culture. Usually, I was the one who turned off the educational or political programs. I was tired of hearing the same old complaints about this politician or that educational philosophy as I was retired and did my thing. He got mad and told me that I had to keep an open mind. And those were the times when I realized one of the gifts Bob had given me— he forced me to focus on someone other than myself. While it was true that I had to change some deeply desired plans to stay with him, he helped make me appreciate that freedom is where the mind takes you and not where the body goes. But I still wanted to see the world!

A Breath of Fresh Air

I could travel again! I made professional strides as well. In 1993, I went to China with forty-four Americans and Canadians for two weeks with a company called "People to People," located in Tacoma, Washington. The program was initiated by President Eisenhower so we could become acquainted with Third World countries. The irony, of course, is that Americans feel we are somehow more advanced than the Chinese.

The Chinese were wonderful hosts and hostesses. We shared our theater secrets and ways to encourage their students and vice versa. We were anxious to take our students there, and they were just as anxious to come to the States. We tried to collaborate on applying and getting grants to go there and vice versa. I was never a tea drinker, but it was a wonderful way to share our thoughts and compare notes. Since we had thirteen hosts in various schools— Beijing, Hangzhou, and Shanghai—it was suggested that we each present them with a gift. I gave a lot of costume theater books, plus items and appropriate books for children's theater. Who would have thought that I would be touring the Forbidden Garden and the Great Wall of China, or be walking along the Yangtze River? We did so much shopping because the cloisonné items, scarves, wall hangings, and silk rugs were cheap, and why not?

The following year, I attended a conference in Russia with all sorts of art and music therapists. I was allowed to do a workshop based on the television program, where I also was the associate producer, *Art for All: Art for People with Disabilities*. We interviewed visual and performing artists with disabilities. I always loved the early Russian history, especially that of Peter the Great, and, of course, the history of the Tsars. It was strange to view the body of Lenin in the Kremlin. And to think that he was embalmed a long, long time ago was also mind boggling.

Touring the Hermitage was awesome because I always think the Metropolitan Museum of Art has so much until you see what other museums have acquired. I thought it was odd that the windows of the museum were dirty and considered sending a case of Windex to them. My mom would be very proud that I actually realized the importance of having clean windows in one of the many arguments we had of "What's the difference if there's little spot on them?" You know, the rationalization, if the windows are not clean, what about the rest of the house? Seeing the *Nutcracker* there in the summer was awesome because I always associate the ballet with Russia, and they performed in the States as a Christmas specialty, not the summer.

We don't realize how lucky we Americans are until we visit other countries like Russia. Then, one hospital closed for a month in May in order to conserve fuel for the winter. Another had a few beds for the hundreds of children in that area. Thankfully, today, there are no longer bread lines as in the past, and the Russian economy was such that people flocked to stores to buy the latest electronic equipment. Today, there are numerous upscale places to shop or to eat at.

I finally graduated with a Ph.D. in educational theater in 1997. I threw myself a party to celebrate a new beginning without the deadlines of this degree. I could now pursue my dreams of becoming a writer and playwright. Costume designing was a thing of the past because I realized that if I continued with designing, there would be no time to finish a dissertation. If nothing else, I wanted a book with my name on it. I had it by May 1997. It was entitled, *Costume Designer Patricia Zipprodt: Her Contribution to the American Theater.*

This thesis explains our craft. I was motivated by the many actors who did not understand what the costume designer did for a living. For some actors, it was hard to comprehend that the playwright's theme, and/or the director's concept, set the pattern for the show. Many thought that if the play was set today, they could wear whatever fashions they liked or looked good on them. In fact, many designers refused to work with certain performers who gave them a hard time. Once designers were established, they could pick and choose their shows. I was also able to attend the conferences as before on costume design, educational theater, and playwriting.

I flew to London quite often to see as many plays as I could to inspire my own playwriting. The English theaters had more matinees to see than the Americans. It was wonderful. I didn't have to consider having only a Saturday or Wednesday. Also, when I went during December or January, I saw children's productions in the morning. At the same time, I researched another costume designer I discovered while writing my thesis on Zipprodt—Sir Percy Anderson. Although it was crazy bussing or tubing it from one part of London to the other, I was ecstatic. Even if the shows were sold out, I went to the theater anyway because someone always returned a ticket, and I was lucky enough to buy it as a "resale." Everything in my life was falling into place again. I was getting back to what I wanted to do.

I made Bob his lasagna or veal parmigiana. I labeled and packaged the choices with directions on when to take the food out of the freezer, and how long to heat them up. I had my cousins Nettie or Joanne, or friends Suzanne or Marie, call him every day. My brother smiled when he realized he only had to heat the food up without cooking anything.

"Ah, man's best friend, the microwave," he said, smiling. But I wasn't happy that Bob wouldn't travel. Bob still refused to take more than two weeks of vacation because he felt he had to work. In my heart, I felt that it had to change.

Vacations with Bob

In the mid-'90s, Bob finally agreed to go away on a vacation with me in the only way I knew he'd agree—I promised to foot the bill. The twenty-dollar man's eyes lit up at the chance for something for nothing.

"I don't have to pay, right? It's a free vacation? Great!"

Bob claimed that money did not like to leave his wallet. The bills were cozy where they were. When he traveled with my Dad and Uncle Frank, Dad would complain that Bob loved to find a place to have breakfast by himself and that they had to wait for him to come back before they went out to eat. Dad also was annoyed that nothing was too expensive for Bob, if someone else were footing the bill. Bob loved ordering lobster whenever he could, especially in Cape Cod.

With me, we're not talking about a week at a time. We're talking about three days and two nights. The Cape was out because I was not driving six to eight hours for a lobster just to turn around the next day. There were good lobster dinners not that far and in less time. At that time, lobsters were not his favorite meal. It was usually steak or veal or chicken parmigiana. But three days and two nights! Ah, well, a nip is better than none. We ventured to Newport, Rhode Island, and stayed at the Marriott Hotel, which cost about 200 dollars each for the rooms—and this was September! It was a beautiful weekend, complete with a tour of the estates, beaches, and shops. We ate in different restaurants and thoroughly enjoyed ourselves. As long as the atmosphere was good, he sat there complacently, waiting to be served.

Bob knew that I wanted to be a playwright. The following year, before we ventured to Mystic, Connecticut, we drove to nearby Waterford, the site of Eugene O'Neill's wonderful, eerie-looking, massive homestead. We went two years in a row, driving through the thickest fogs and downpours.

"I think I hear the foghorns. I think we're in a scene from one of O'Neill's sea plays that I costumed at NYU," I said as we drove closer to the estate.

"This place is spooky. Look! The homestead is closed, and no one is around to give us any information. Even the ghosts seemed to be vacationing elsewhere, don't you think?"

"You got me!" Bob answered grimly. "It's spooky and weird to say the least. Maybe you can contact the ghost? Wooooo, wooooo. Where are you?"

"Ha, ha!" I answered with a smirk on my face.

Undiscouraged, we discovered O'Neill's childhood's home in New London, not too far from Mystic, the following year. What were the odds that the home was opened to the public the next day instead of the day we showed up?

"Rosalie, read all the information you can find on this guy and read all his plays. That's much better than all these wild goose chases every year, don't you think? I mean, he's dead, right?" Bob, as usual, could be very philosophical and practical at times.

"You're right, of course. I can't disagree with you today."

Instead, we focused our travels on discovering the ins and outs of Mystic and the neighboring towns. Mystic has a charming boat ride that sailed around a small area, with no waves or storms to contend with, just beautiful estates to ogle at as the boat made its way around the inlet. Bob insisted that he got boat sick but survived with no problems and had a good time. He also got used to my shopping from one store to another. If he didn't feel like shopping, he became a product and people watcher. His first complaint was that the shops did not carry the variety that the New York stores offered, and were boring. Of course, much of it was country or New England style decor. He offered some comments on the clothes that were worn or bought here.

"New Yorkers are more sophisticated. Don't waste your money," he'd say. Regarding household goods, he advised, "How many more sets of water glasses or tablecloths do we need?" He certainly didn't complain when I bought him Ralph Lauren shirts. At another time, I bought three watercolors—all seascapes. They didn't fit into the artwork I had on the walls in the house, so I put them in his room over his desk.

"What do you think about the watercolors?" I asked.

"Are you telling me that if I stand too close to these, I'll sail away?" was his reply.

Sometimes it was hard to tell whether he was not feeling well or was just yanking my chain with his odd sense of humor.

One year, Bob informed me that he usually read the travel section of *The New York Daily News* and thought it would be a good idea to go to a resort in Salisbury, Connecticut, which was not too far from the Berkshires. While a hurricane passed through the day before we planned to leave, we decided to go on up anyway. The hotel we booked was old, quaint, and charming. My room was located in the main building. Bob still smoked at the time, so he was given a room in the guesthouse, which had a set of straight line up steps to his room, á la turn-of-the-century decor.

"I'll never get up and come down again," he moaned.

"Give up smoking," I said.

Of course, he ignored what I said. We met later to tour the area and ate in a noted restaurant. As we pulled up to the place, I said, "What a great place!"

"A dump," Bob answered.

I didn't realize at that time that he only liked modern hotels and modern restaurants. Turn-of-the-century places turned him off. For the remainder of the weekend, we toured Edith Walton's home and the Norman Rockwell Museum, and then found quaint cafes for lunch and craft stores in which to browse. Bob brought up as many newspapers as he could find, while I couldn't resist buying Christmas items and gifts because they were unusual. At last, we were both able to indulge our whimsies.

On the last night, I booked reservations at our hotel for dinner under the name "Dr. Contino." When we walked in, the hostess led us to a beautifully set table with candles for a romantic evening. Bob and I laughed hysterically and explained to the hostess that we were brother and sister, and then asked to reserve the table for other guests. She was pleasantly surprised since very few people traveled with siblings.

The next day, we drove home in good spirits, remembering what roads not to take again with its many, many trees. I complimented Bob on his choice of place. At least, he was taking an interest in traveling even if it was only for a short time. Our vacations were still regimented to three days and two nights; that was our routine. When Bob traveled with my father and uncle, it was for two to three weeks. My friends thought, that since I threatened to leave my brother at a resort when he got his nanny up, he preferred his schedule.

I gave up trying to convince him otherwise because no matter how I tried, he would only answer, "I am an American-born citizen who loves America and only want to travel in America."

Twice a year, three days and two nights was better than nothing. At least, it was a change of scenery.

What If I Wasn't There?

As a teacher, you're always a page ahead of the class, but once my brother had retired, I was never a page ahead when it came to his ongoing need for medical attention. There were always *more*—more doctors, more tests, more new medications, and more rules to follow. I could never be prepared in advance for things and specialties and drugs I did not even know existed before I walked through the doctor's office door.

Bob was a heavy smoker for more than forty years. Contrary to his claim of having three to four cigarettes a day, it was roughly three to four packs of cigarettes a day. His hands were stained nicotine yellow. The cuffs of all his coats and raincoats, even his prized eight-hundred-dollar Burberry raincoat were rimmed with burn marks.

Bob's careless health habits caught up with him with a vengeance in 1997 when he was hospitalized for the first time. The laundry list of ailments included: pneumonia, hypertension, high cholesterol, emphysema, asthma, and congestive heart failure. The intern in the emergency room in Maimomides Hospital insisted that Bob was an alcoholic. I kept screaming that he didn't drink. The two of us arguing at the top of our lungs must have made quite a picture. Finally, I gave up in exasperation and told my brother that I would visit him the next day. When I did, he was sitting up and babbling complaints.

"You have no idea what *I* went through! They raced me from floor to floor for one test after another. I am damn lucky that I didn't get motion sickness. It was like being on a boat on a stretcher. This is your fault because you gave me these health problems. I was healthy before that."

The doctor came in at that moment and informed that the MRI showed no stroke and that Bob's lungs were clear. He immediately cautioned us that this did not mean Bob wasn't gravely ill. He had all the medical problems mentioned above, but was stable for the moment. He suggested no smoking and a salt-free diet, and should follow his orders for a healthier lifestyle. My brother, as usual, smiled and thanked him. But as I came to know his "thank you for your concern attitude" or "will do" or "tell my sister," the doctor's comments meant very little to him until much later.

"What do you think I am, a Rockette?" he snapped unfortunately, when a female doctor asked him to lift his leg.

Mortified, I stifled a laugh and just rolled my eyes. At least, he still had a sense of humor. However, he was also annoying and insulting because he referred to every female as a nurse or an aide even if I chided him and pointed out that they were female doctors. He was insistent that females could not be doctors. Whether he really was that sexist and out of touch, or whether he just wanted to get a rise out of his sister earning a doctoral degree is something I will never know for sure.

Who knew at the time when I was finishing my doctorate that caring for Bob would become my next major project?

Life and a Doctorate

Bob shares a laugh with Suzanne Plavé at my
graduation party for my PHD in 1997

In September 1996, cousin Raffi passed away, and his sister, Palma, soon
followed him, the following year. NYU was threatening to throw me out
because I still hadn't finished my doctorate. I was already there for sixteen
years as a student. That summer, two professors left my committee. When you
work on a doctorate, there are three professors who are on your committee.
One is the chair and the other two serve on the committee. Two are from your
field and one is from an outside subject. Dr. Perkinson taught history of
education. I had asked him to serve with the understanding that he might not

have any interest whatsoever in costume design, but would just have to concern himself with the quality of the research. He had stayed but was now retired. Now, I wrote another request—my "Portia's plea of mercy letter," as I called it. He responded and promised not to strand me. At least, he didn't live too far—just in nearby New Jersey. The other professor from my program was on his way to a new assignment in Arizona. I still needed a committee member who lived closer. The newest member of the educational theater program, Dr. Alistair Martin-Smith, couldn't give me a commitment, as he had to read the dissertation first. But that changed when Alistair informed me that his wife was a costume designer, but he never knew what she did exactly, and that it was probably time he found out. Thank goodness! After reconstituting the committee, I promised all three members that I would finish the dissertation and graduate in 1997.

When Bob was discharged from the hospital, he was told the usual: a salt-free diet, and stop smoking. I knew I could cook the right thing for dinner but had no idea what he was eating breakfast and lunch once he left the house each morning for work. Guys don't normally share their eating habits with gal folks.

Two years later, he was hospitalized for the same problems, and, once again, he was asked to follow a salt-free diet and stop smoking. Bob continued to have that hacking cigarette cough when he walked down the street. His nightly routine didn't change either. My brother slept a few hours in his bed each night, then woke up at three or four in the morning, went downstairs, and slept in the upright Queen Anne chair. He couldn't sleep lying down for too many hours as he could not breathe. He didn't have to tell me because I heard him: *How could I sleep? I was going to the gym to work off steam.* But nothing changed his mind. Following medical orders was not part of my Bob's makeover or path to recovery for his own good. He smoked and ate whenever and whatever he wanted.

By 2001, several problems arose at work. Bob had a hard time walking because he limped more, and it was not getting better. The bosses were afraid to send him anywhere because they felt he would get hit by a moving vehicle, and they would feel guilty and might even be legally responsible. The bosses didn't need his death on their consciences or in their insurance claims. The new water pill that was prescribed to reduce the hypertension worked so fast that he urinated in his pants before he got to work and was sent home because his clothes reeked. We were dedicated visitors at the doctor's office. I begged this HMO doctor to change or give my brother a lighter dosage. My request was turned down because the doctor insisted that he had to take the medication since the hypertension was life-threatening. There were no second choices.

I sorely missed my uncle's advice. He was a doctor and often helped me make informed decisions before he passed away in 1981. His philosophy was that medicines should be kept to a minimum to avoid side effects. At the time, I was furious at my brother's doctor's lack of understanding, though some of that may have been fear and frustration of just not knowing if there were alternatives. Some women complain about their biological clock ticking and ebbing away. Bob's life clock was ticking away. He was not getting better, and I felt that I was watching his health go down the tubes.

Adding to the frustrations were Bob's stubbornness and capriciousness. When Bob refused to go to the hospital, I begged him to change health plans because I knew the doctors in my plan, but nothing moved him. He didn't like his doctors but didn't want mine either. Perhaps there was a reason for why he refused help, though I never understood why he wouldn't change. To complicate the situation, he once took matters into his own hands and switched the prescriptions that he considered beneficial to him and discarded the others. His health was worse than before.

I knew that in order to maintain my own health and sanity, I had to get away. In the middle of June, I went to a writer's conference in Wesleyan, Connecticut. One of the perks was to submit some writing to get feedback. Little did I know that this writing would be finished and published in 2007 as *Born to Create*. It was about my resolve to go back to school at age forty to fulfill my dreams. I chose Roxanna Robinson who is described as the voice and storyteller of the WASP group. (I read many of her works and don't see any difference between her community and mine.) She was very encouraging in suggesting that I "slow down" the chapters and put in more details; I did.

On the way back, I stopped for dinner at Chuck's Steak House in Darien. I knew that my brother liked Steak Delmonico, so I bought one to take home for him. When I arrived home, I could not awaken him and was terrified.

"Why am I so tired?" he asked.

I told him to stop all the medication and we would go to the doctor on Monday morning. Nothing was changed and nothing was resolved; the medication stayed the same. My brother was still being sent home from work. Bob's health worsened. A new chest X-ray revealed that his lungs were congested. He refused to go to the hospital. Whenever I mentioned the local hospital, he would say, "Mom, Dad, Raffi, Palma."

"What are you saying?"

"I'm naming all the relatives who died there."

"Don't be ridiculous. We took Dad home. Besides, they were old and sickly, and if you don't take care of yourself, you're next. You have to change your lifestyle to be healthier and live longer."

"Yeah, yeah, yeah."

Nothing changed his mind.

"I can't breathe, I can't breathe. Help me! Help me! Mama! Mama!" I heard over and over, during the day or night.

Was this call for help an expression that just fell out of his body without his ever hearing it? I didn't know then and still don't know today. One day, we went for a haircut and a shave. My brother could hardly walk. When the barber escorted Bob to the car and helped him to get in there, I started to cry. This was a man who could walk fast and be on his own. I remembered when we got caught in a downpour in Essex, Connecticut.

"We're all wet! The water is up to our ankles!" I yelled as we ran from the car to the hotel.

He shouted, "So what? Rain is good for you. It makes you strong and beautiful!"

"Yeah, right," I answered, "and to catch pneumonia, too!"

Later that day, I drove him to the nearest hospital and left him there. I went home and cried. An hour later, the doorbell rang. It was Bob. He refused to go to any hospital because no matter what I told him, Bob felt he would die there. With the exception of Dad, he knew that all our other relatives died in the hospital. I tried to explain that they were older and sicker.

By October 1, 2002, I finally convinced my brother to switch to GHI medical plans.

"If nothing else," I said, "I'll save your life by a year. Get it?"

"Got it."

Bob knew I was fed up with this nonsense of getting nowhere with his health.

At least, I had more control of the doctors to see whose reputations were good and reliable. I couldn't understand how we could visit his doctor month after month and have the same medications prescribed with no improvements. Bob and I went to my primary doctor, Dr. Paul Maravel, who was younger, a true professional and ahead of the game. The doctor outlined a plan.

Step 1: He prescribed a blood test. Based on that information, our new routine included visits to kidney specialists who thought my brother was a candidate for dialysis—three times a week and then some. *Oh, God. Oh, no, please,* I thought. Thank heaven, Bob listened, stuck to the prescribed medications, and changed his diet. He still didn't smoke anymore, and those services were never needed. The kidney specialist prescribed X-rays of his kidneys, as well as an abdominal sonogram. This was the beginning of a nightmare for me. One of those super gems.

"I'm not pregnant! This is an outrage!" Bob screamed at the imaging place while he was being examined. The petite technician was at her wits' end. She called me in because she couldn't keep him quiet. He couldn't sit back and wouldn't sit still. I was mortified as I thought we would be thrown out. I hoped that no one recognized me because I also went to this hospital for tests and X-rays. My creative brain designed a hood to cover my face so that no one would recognize me. Sadly, it went no further than an idea. I hoped no one in the waiting room knew me. The technician called in two tall technicians to assist her. They sat Bob up and back. That shut him up temporarily. After all that, Bob needed to have the kidney stones blasted. As I sat and waited for him from one doctor's office or medical center, I started writing notes and commented on what was going on and Bob's reactions, as well as mine, to the whole situation.

At the same time, because we switched medical plans, he was no longer covered for the NYS Mental Health Program. I was recommended to a neurologist who took him off Haldol and prescribed Zoloft, another antidepressant instead. We also went to a wonderful cardiologist, Dr. Bo Shim, who was able to give him an EKG in the office. My brother carried on because he couldn't lie back. However, the technician was pleasant, a capable and true professional who was able to get enough information for the doctor to read. The cardiologist realized that my brother would not be an easy candidate for the stress test now because he had difficulty lying down and his breathing was laborious. That procedure was tabled for a future time. We now visited the cardiologist four times a year.

"How do you feel?" he asked my brother every time we visited him.

"Fine. Never felt better. Can you help me up, please?" Mr. Denial spoke crispy and clearly.

Maybe he was scared that he would have to be hospitalized again for a long time. He'd rather be in a state of denial than to confide on how he really felt. When he was younger, he was sent there. He was now older and wanted no part of it.

"You have your hands full. Good luck!" said the doctor with a knowing smile.

On Thursday, in the third week of January 2003, we made an appointment with the kidney specialist to have the stones blasted—a day in, day out procedure. Once home, my brother refused to take the antibiotics. But, at least, I felt we were stabilizing the situation.

Then one day, Bob flew down the stairs, screaming, "Help me! Help me!" I called 911.

The Caregiver

We were back at Victory Memorial Hospital again. He's running a temperature of 105 degrees. The hospital doctor chewed me out because I didn't give him the antibiotics.

"Get real," I answered. "He's sixty-two years old!"

The hospitalization was a blessing in disguise. He also had gall stones in the bile duct and an enlarged, infected gall bladder, plus a huge growth of liquefied fat the size of a grapefruit in his abdomen. Everything was removed, and biopsies were taken and tested for cancer. The infection was still raging in his system. The hospital also monitored his heart, as he had congestive heart failure. I never knew what room or floor my brother was in or on because they upgraded his condition each day. I was running back and forth to the house as the workers finished sealing up the walls. After they left, I welcomed the next team in—the rug cleaning specialists.

Bob was hospitalized for three weeks before the infection finally cleared up. The lab tests came back. No cancer! What a relief! Bob was discharged, a day after a horrific snowstorm, with a walker, an aide, new medications, a physical therapist, a visiting nurse, and a health aide, a godsend named Charlotte. She was an efficient and an extremely caring person, who handled my brother with tender loving care. We had many aides in the past, first for my father and now for Bob. Her grandson recently graduated from Shell Bank Junior High where I taught. What were the odds on that? Of course, I retired in 1991, he attended several years later and recently returned from Iraq.

Hopefully, we prayed for a better life. The kidney specialist checked Bob out once or twice and asked to be seen in six months. We visited the doctor who operated on his gall bladder. He took out the stitches and gave Bob a clean bill of health. No more visits to him. Thank you for small favors!

The eye doctor's visit was a pleasant and calming event. With the new prescription in hand, I purchased two new pairs of glasses for Bob that he tried on, liked, and promised to wear. The hearing doctor said that my brother should have a hearing aid because he had a punctured eardrum. I was surprised that he wasn't more than half deaf as, for years, he cleaned his ears with the ends of matchsticks. Bob bolted from the chair and yelled out to Charlotte and me:

"No, I don't! See you guys outside!"

A visit to Dr. Robert Miele, the podiatrist, was another screaming fit. It took four people to get him to soak his feet in the small vat. Thank God, Dr. Miele agreed to make house visits every few months. Bob was pleasant and pleased when he came as it meant another service for his needs. The king wins again. When Bob developed cysts in the groin area, the vascular specialist informed me that Bob had these throughout his body, and that they were inherited. I recalled Mom having them on her knees when we were kids. Amazing what idiosyncrasies you have as offshoots from your parents.

During his recuperation at home from gall bladder surgery, my brother showed everyone his scar.

"My sister's scar," meaning me. "My sister caused me to have a scar on my perfectly formed body."

"Oh, please," said I. "Get real."

We have a tub shower. He couldn't or wouldn't lift his leg to shower because of the scar. I offered to buy him whatever chair he needed to sit in that shower. He refused. The aide, Charlotte Grosso, was hired permanently, out-of-pocket, to take care of my brother. Little did I know that she would become an important part of the family. Whenever he refused to go to a procedure or visit a doctor, Charlotte had a calming effect on him and explained the situation to him. Service, nothing but service! As far as he was concerned, I was the witch who loved doctors and calling 911. Bob had difficulty walking down the steps for weeks after he was discharged. Gradually, as he healed and felt confident and stronger, and with Charlotte by his side, he walked down the steps and went for a walk to the corner five houses away and not in the other directions, a city block to the corner. He went from a walker, to a quad, to a cane.

Bob, too, usually went to the barber twice a week for a shave and/or haircut. Since he couldn't go out for long periods of time, we hired the barber from the hospital to come to the house instead. My brother gave up shaving himself years before because he said his hands weren't as steady as they were before. I didn't question it. Usually, he went twice a week on his own to any barber who did shaves. When he felt up to it, I drove him and Charlotte to the nearest barber in Bay Ridge that we thought had a truly professional staff. Some of these establishments hired people that were for the birds. A half hour later, I picked them up and did what Bob wanted to do—eat out, buy CDs, or go home. When Bob looked a little down, I bought him more Ralph Lauren shirts and sweaters to cheer him up. As usual, the main complaint was that the shirts didn't have any pockets. So big deal! Keep your glasses in your pants' pocket!

When he wasn't up to par to dine out, he ordered from the nearby Ravioli Fair Deli or Pizza Den. In the past, this was a weekend treat for him. Once he had retired, he loved to order lunch most of the week. My neighbors always got a kick out of it because they would say, "Ravioli Fair or Pizza Den visited your house today." That suited me fine, as I was never a breakfast or lunch person. Bob loved to make his own lunch or order it already made. I okayed it because the food was good and nutritious. If he preferred cold cuts, I shopped at Waldbaum's for low sodium meats with whole wheat, rye, or grain bread. No more junk foods for him.

Bob continued to say, "Help me! Help me!" for some reason, all day long, and then would deny saying it.

"Never said a word. I know you. You can't wait to take me to another doctor or call 911," he responded sarcastically when I asked why.

"You should be happy that I am here and willing to do that, luv!" I answered back.

We did go to another doctor, this time an orthopedic surgeon who informed me that my brother needed a hip replacement. Bob refused to consider surgery, so the surgeon prescribed physical therapy at Lutheran Hospital's offsite place in Bay Ridge. Bob gave them a run for the money during the thirty-two times we frequented the place. The treatment didn't help because he wouldn't or couldn't work with the therapist no matter how cordially and carefully they treated him. In fact, it became a comedy routine because Bob spent more time demanding his cane.

Everyone in the place yelled out in unison, "No!"

One of the problems was that Bob was fearful of sitting on a stationary bike. I tried to calm him down.

"What's wrong with you? It's stationary."

"I don't care. I never had a bike when I grew up!"

I looked at him stunned. *How stupid*, I thought. This bike was going nowhere. It was stationary, but he was right! He didn't. He only had a tricycle until he outgrew it. I recalled that neither one of us had bikes when we grew up. A few years ago, I asked my mother why they didn't buy me a bike. I had to borrow every friend's bike instead.

"Daddy and I decided that if we did and you were hit by a car, it would be the fault of the person who bought the bike," she said.

I couldn't believe I heard it right. My friends and I were great roller skaters and played street hockey. Our childhood friend Marie's Dad made us hockey sticks and gave us a puck. We drew oblong lines sewer to sewer for "our skating rink." The sewers were the goalposts. We played for hours, in and out of traffic. We were a true driver's nightmare. I am so thankful that Mom never saw us skating. We never would have had fun then.

Recently, I realized that my brother and I were products of older parents. My Mom was twenty-eight when I was born and Dad, thirty-five. When Bob was born, she was thirty or thirty-one and Dad, thirty-seven. Today, many of my friends who married older had the same attitude as my parents. They're overcareful and watch their children like hawks.

Despite the aggravation from Bob, and no matter how gently the staff tried to help him, it was no use. These sessions were pleasant experiences because everyone was caring and very professional. To placate him, we would go out and eat lunch in a different restaurant or drive to the Barnes & Noble on Staten Island for the latest CDs. After going to Lutheran's offsite location for physical therapy, we faced another problem. Bob had to pay a fifteen-dollar co-payment. For some reason, he was getting billed as if he never had insurance. Finally, I called Lutheran Billing Department to see what the story was. It was all a matter of putting in the right codes to GHI. It was a two-way process of getting it right. Bob now owed nothing. I wrote a letter to the boss of the woman who helped us, as every little plus in life deserved a reward. It was scary when I think of it. If I didn't take care of it, my brother would have left the letters there and could have been sued for nonpayment. This had to be a gift of love!

I made an appointment with another orthopedic surgeon for a second opinion, and he informed me that Bob could not have his hip replaced because he was not a compliant patient. He was too fidgety. When people have hip surgery, they must sit still, not cross their legs or walk fast; otherwise, the hip slips out of place, a problem that required more surgery. Having more therapy was out of the question. His hip was shot. However, I thought Bob would kiss the doctor because it meant he couldn't have the surgery. That was a hard one for me to swallow because that was not part of Bobby's physical and mental state at this time. My brother would suffer whatever pains he had for the rest of his life. I knew that his hip hurt because there were times when he couldn't sit still in the car and leaned on me as I drove. A little hard at times, as Bob was almost six feet tall, and I am much shorter.

We also frequented the office of the pulmonary specialist. Since she was a well-known doctor, her office was frequently crowded. We had to wait and wait in the reception area. If the time passed when my brother's appointment was scheduled, he asked the receptionist what time he was to see the doctor and why she wasn't on schedule. If we waited a really long time—sometimes two hours or more—he hummed or sang a song.

"Let him be because we don't blame him," the patients whispered to me.

Bob sat there nodding in agreement. "See how they know better than you, little sister of mine," he said. "You're always ready to have me face the knife. You lose this time."

Mum was the word for me because if I dared say anything, he would come out with some crude, obnoxious remark directed at me. These doctor visits were beginning to get to him, no matter how many times I explained that if he took care of himself, this wouldn't have happened. We're half Calabrese Italian-Americans, which means that we are known to be thickheaded—*capa tosta*. I think it's safe to say that Bob made up for a thousand Calabrese.

The doctor had two examining rooms. As she examined one patient, the other waited for her to finish and come in. Bob gave her "a what for," too. He refused to sit on the examining table, and, when she came in, commented:

"Oh, you finally arrived. We thought we weren't good enough for you. I'm in very good health, so let's make this fast."

He wasn't, and she prescribed a nebulizer to be used three times a day to clear up the congestion she heard in his lungs. This was a wonderful invention, because on humid days, he was able to use it up to six times a day without any problems. The medication she prescribed was not as heavy duty as the HMO primary care doctor gave. Bob did not fall asleep as before and was more alert. Since he was not a compliant patient for her, too, she accommodated his needs and restlessness. Instead of sitting in her office, she sent a PA (physician assistant) every six weeks, a wonderful human being whom Bob liked to talk to when he came. Blood tests were also being done at home to avoid waiting many hours at the lab. I thanked her for her professionalism and her patience.

"I can see that he gives you a run for the money."

Sadly, no matter how many times I thought we were finished with doctors, there was always another medical problem to deal with always, another test or MRI to take or another medication to try. There was no end to this merry-go-round of specialists. I was never a page ahead.

Although he was only sixty-three, it seemed as though one part of his system was going after another. With all the traumas he put me through to help him, he never complained of any pains in his body. Weird! Just weird! When he could stand sitting in the car longer than an hour, we drove to Chuck's Steakhouse in Darien. I also bought some of their New York strip steaks for him and filet mignons for me to cook at home. I invited people to eat out with us, and had more dinner gatherings instead of parties. I gave up the parties because I saw he was changing and had no patience. I didn't need to be insulted over some stupid comment and have screaming matches with a house full of guests.

I found other places to have a brunch or lunch, such as the Tuscan Restaurant at the Marriott Hotel in Bridgewater Common in New Jersey. It was a wonderful and calm place in a beautifully decorated hotel. We had many dinners with our friends, Cathy and Marie, at Kennedy's in Breezy Point, Queens. We were such frequent visitors at both places that we were greeted as old friends, which pleased my brother very much. He was happy that he could have a conversation with them as well.

Bob, of course, told everyone who would listen, that his sister got a thrill out of calling 911 because she had a fetish about doctors. I reminded my brother that I taught English to one hundred forty kids; that only a few were nutty; and that I survived. He was the only human being who made me totally nuts. To myself, I wondered if I were totally sane. I questioned why I promised my parents I would take care of him as I was wearing thin. We were arguing constantly no matter how I tried to keep my cool. At least, most of the arguments were at home when the two of us were alone.

Since my "free" time was now limited, whatever new plays, short stories, or poems I wrote, I rewrote and sent out. During the last few years, I didn't travel far unless I took him because I feared I would find him dead when I came home. My window of freedom got smaller and smaller; no more traveling to Europe or anywhere else unless it was nearby. Let's face it. No matter how many people I hired, I was still the sister and the one responsible for him. I became a teacher because of Mom's wise reasoning.

"Forget being a secretary. You hate typing! Forget being a nurse! You have no patience, and the patient will have jumped out of the window with your sense of compassion!"

She should have added that when I wished to push him off the porch, I wanted to jump off the porch myself sometimes.

Life on Hold

In 2002, I had the electrical wiring changed. In 2003, unfortunately, there was a leak from the top of the outside steps to the beautiful new electrical box under the steps. The first row of the panel was wet, and the electrician switched the line to offset it in order for us to have air conditioning. I was concerned about the safety element, but the electrician assured me that it was safe. I felt confident and attended the Pi Lambda Theta Educational Honor Society Conference held twelve miles south of Boston as part of poster session, "Writing a Monologue." The hotel wasn't that far from home, and I thought I'd take a chance. At 5:30 p.m. I called my brother to check in. No answer. I called, called, and called again. No answer. I called my tenants to check up on him, but they didn't see him downstairs, although they did see the air conditioner on full blast. I was furious because he was supposed to shut off the air conditioner before going to bed. I called the electrician to check the electrical boxes. Everything was okay. I called my brother at 3:30 A.M., because I figured that if he went to bed early, he would get up early. I was right. I casually asked if he turned off the air.

"Of course, just before I went to sleep. Stop the worrying."

Sure, I thought. At 9:00 A.M., I called back when Charlotte was there.

"I'd better turn off the air. Otherwise, my sister will yell."

She laughed when he told her. She informed him that he would do it only when he goes to sleep upstairs and not while he was downstairs. That was the last time I ventured anywhere overnight without Bob. The stress was too great on my nerves. I was convinced that my brother knew how to keep-me-in-line, and not stray from serving him and have a life of my own. For the first time, I was grateful that I wasn't married and had a husband or kids to contend with. I knew what a lot of my friends went through if I'd had to make a decision, too, of who was more important—him or them. I cried in my hotel room until it was time for me to be downstairs for a meeting with the rest of the Region I group, and I cried all the way home. Why was I so upset? I worried about that electrical box. My dad once had a terrible dream that Bobby was on fire. It might be superstitious to think it was prophetic, but it is better to be superstitious than grief-stricken.

In August, I had better luck. I was part of the AATE (American Alliance for Theater in Education) committee that was having their convention this year at the Marriott Hotel in New York City. It was my saving grace. We met once a month to judge and accept the proposals that were mailed to the committee members. Also, we designated August 1 as an NYU Day, whereby the whole day was dedicated to having plays performed at the campus to show off our theater resources and productions. This included the University Theater in the Education Building, the Black Box Theater in the Pless Building, The Provincetown Playhouse on MacDougal Street, and the space used by CAT (Creative Arts Team NYU now part of CUNY) on Broadway.

We had a lot of fun working on this event because the day presented an opportunity for participants to see what NYU had to offer and what other events were happening in the area. Sadly, since 9/11, Lower Broadway suffered from a lack of tourism. Business has picked up, but when we shopped in the boutiques, the owners told us it could be better. In the middle of the day, many of us opted to go to the CTA's (Children's Theater Association) luncheon at Sardi's Restaurant to welcome and greet familiar faces and not so familiar faces from my field to New York City. My own lecture/demo was scheduled for August 3—probably the last slot in the conference. It became a joke that, as friends, they were waving "good-bye" to me and New York, while I was smiling "hello" to the participants of my lecture demo on Percy Anderson, turn-of-the-century British costume designer. At least, I felt rewarded and was not wasting my precious time totally speaking to these costume designers.

In 2004, I had better luck. My lecture on Leonard Covello, an Italian-born educator, was accepted as part of the Region I Pi Lambda Theta Conference. The NYU Rho Chapter served as host at the Diplomat Hotel in Lower Manhattan and also on the NYU campus. Covello fought to have the language of Italian accepted as part of the high school curriculum in the 1920s and was the first principal of Benjamin Franklin High School (now called the Academy of Math and Science) in East Harlem. He himself always lived in East Harlem when it was a strong Italian community. As time went on, the population changed and the area became a Puerto Rican and Dominican community. Today the area is known as Spanish Harlem. Covello had the high school designated as a twenty-four hour school, with speakers to inform the parents and students about their culture—not only Puerto Ricans, but other ethnic groups who attended the high school as well. He didn't want them to be in the dark about their heritage as the Italians were when they came to America. Daniel Moynihan and Vito Marcantonio were students of the school who worked with Fiorello La Guardia for better housing and equal rights when they graduated.

Bob and I managed to go away for the weekend to Connecticut, as usual—our favorite state. We didn't drive as far north as we usually did. Usually, we left bright and almost early on Saturday but this time decided to head out on Friday. The traffic, the touring, and shopping took its toll on Bob's health because there were too many hours spent in the car. He slept twelve hours through the night. I left it up to him if he wanted to stay another night. He said he'd rather go home. I was glad because he was pale and drawn. I knew his hip hurt by the way he practically sat on me as I drove home. I knew I couldn't ask him how he felt as he would lash out of my loving doctors and 911.

Labor Day has been a harbinger of bad health news for both my father and brother. On the day before the holiday, Charlotte and my brother went upstairs. Two minutes later, Charlotte came down to tell me that Bob wasn't responding.

"To what?" I asked. I ran upstairs and saw that Bob was out cold. I called 911 immediately.

As I gave the 911 operator my name and address, she said, "Between Eighty-Sixth Street and Benson Avenue?"

"Yes," I answered. I started to give her the telephone number but she finished it for me. *Oh, my God,* I thought. I figured they knew us because we called so much since 1997. The ambulance quickly arrived and my brother was taken to Victory Memorial Hospital in less than a half hour. I followed with an updated list of my brother's medications. The doctors couldn't figure out what was wrong.

At first, they thought Bob had diabetes because the sugar content was so high and tested his blood every few hours. They reviewed the medications he was on and told me to stop the Zoloft because of the sugar content. They ordered more tests and MRIs of his body. When I visited Bob the next day, I asked the male nurse how he did on the tests. He informed me that my brother refused to take them.

"Why did you listen to him?" I practically shrieked.

"Patients have rights today, so no tests were administered."

I stormed into my brother's room.

"You have no patient rights! Do you hear me? You will go home after you take these tests. Get it?" I said in as calm a manner as I could manage.

"How many MRIs do they need of my head?"

"As many as it needs to see what the problem was."

"You don't understand, I'm being mauled with all these blood tests! I'm plucked every two minutes!"

"Stop complaining. We have to see what the problems are."

Most of the tests were done except for one—with or without me towering over him. The GI specialist removed several polyps from his stomach and said they were inherited too. So what else was new? My family members were long deceased and would not know if any of them had these things. These medical procedures were all part of the new medicine. The GI specialist also thought she saw a problem with the pancreas and liver, and suggested having more tests done once Bob returned home. She was concerned because there was a possibility of pancreatic cancer, but it was hard to tell and recommended further testing. She couldn't perform the tests then because more serious emergencies came into the hospital that evening. Bob was discharged the next morning because procedures for X-rays or MRIs were closed on Sunday and Labor Day. Medical insurance did not pay for unneeded hospital stays. Appointments for the new tests were to be scheduled as soon as possible.

When Bob came home, the ambulance driver informed me that Bob's ear was bleeding. I told the young man that Bob was cleaning his ears with a key. Back we went to the hospital! I followed in my car. When the emergency room saw my expression, they assured me that Bob would be all right. Another antibiotic would do the trick because it was nothing serious. I just glared at my brother. When would I catch a break?

"You owe me big time, brother," I said. Bob shrugged and said nothing.

At home, I called GHI, as it was thought my brother had the beginning of diabetes. They sent us the needles and equipment to monitor his blood. This started a whole new round of arguments with Bob every time we had to check his blood sugar, which was three times per day. I made an appointment with the primary doctor to have the X-rays that *Dr. Sand suggested set up, as well as an appointment with a GI specialist for an colonoscopy. When the test results came in, the prognosis was not good. Bob needed an MRI to further clarify what was going on with his pancreas. I also called the neurologist to tell him the problem with Zoloft. When he didn't return my calls, I made an appointment for my brother to visit another neurologist. I had no time to waste. She was extremely professional, and I was very happy with the questions she asked my brother as she prescribed another medication. She also requested more MRIs on the head, spine, and stomach. Bob and I looked at each other. We just left without saying another word.

I called the family lawyer, Andrew Sichenze, and set up a meeting for "Health Proxies" for Bob and me. He was very considerate and refused to have Bob get out of the car. He sat next to him and had him sign five copies. Bob wrote all over the page. I was furious and mortified.

"I will say a novena for you!" the lawyer yelled as he jumped out of the car.

"What is your problem? Why did you write all over the page? When we get home, practice your handwriting!"

"What lawyer doesn't have me sign at a desk?" Bob said, without giving it much thought.

Charlotte and I burst out laughing.

I made an appointment with the GI doctor for a colonoscopy. Needless to say, if I thought the visit for a sonogram was a circus, little did I know what my brother had in store for me with this visit because Bob was downright rude and crude in that office describing his bowel movements. If the words *humiliated* and *mortified* could be seen in neon lights over my head, they would have shone brightly across the world for all to see. When we left, I screamed like a banshee as to why the hell he was downright disgusting and what the hell was his problem!

"What do you think? How about pizza or Chinese food? Take your pick!" Bob asked.

On October 16, I left Cindy, the cleaning lady, home and went to the office of the All Stars Projects, a group I donate to that encourages inner city kids to audition with their own routines and perform on the stage. No one is rejected. From the All Stars theater/office, we were bused to the Academy of Math and Science in East Harlem to watch the latest groups of enthusiastic future performers. Ironically, this was the school I had been looking for—the former Benjamin Franklin High School where Leonard Covello, the educator, was the first principal of the school.

Later, I figured that between the time the cleaning lady left and I came home, it had to be no more than three hours. Upon coming home, I noticed that the front door was opened. I thought it was odd, until I looked down and saw blood on the tile floor.

"Bobby! Bobby!" I screamed and ran upstairs. Bob was lying on the bed, holding his ear, which was bleeding. "What happened?"

"I don't know. I cut my ear."

I called 911 again. And once again, I followed the ambulance to the hospital with the updated list of medications. The doctors gave Bob some shots to deaden the pain before they stitched up the back of the ear.

"Have mercy on me. Please, have mercy," he screamed over and over until the drug took its effect.

I was numb because I couldn't understand why Bob was afflicted with so many health problems. I sat there stunned and depressed. What did my brother do to deserve these ailments? What did he do to deserve this life? To complicate this night, my arthritic knees were in bad shape, too. Presently, the pain was unbearable. My right knee was singing to me more as if I had three knives slicing through over and over twenty-four hours a day. The hamstrings on both knees were no better. The pain was so excruciating that I couldn't cry if I wanted to. I credited this problem as a reward for being attentive to my brother because the more he got sicker, the more intense the pains were. Originally, one surgeon suggested I have total knee replacements. Surgery was out of the question, as I couldn't leave Bob and go for rehab for two weeks. Let's face it, no matter how many people took care of him, I was still the sister and had to be there. Also, he would be calling me every morning, afternoon, and evening, asking me when was I going to come home and complaining about the food.

I sat on the cot next to him, rubbing my knees over and over. The patient next to me, a gentleman, perhaps around seventy-five years old or so called out.

"I would like some food. I'm hungry. Hello! Is anybody out there?" Then he added sweetly, "Nurse, Nurse, I would like to have something to eat. I'm hungry." He changed his tone of voice. "Nurse, oh, dear, will somebody get me something to eat. I'm very hungry."

"This is like the Twilight Zone. Don't you think?" I asked her.

She didn't answer. A short time later, I thought Bob was ready to go home. He wasn't. The emergency room doctors informed me that he had to stay overnight. Here we go again.

The next morning, I rushed to the hospital once again and met the doctor who took care of him the previous time.

"Hi," I said cheerily. "We're back! We missed seeing you."

"We're checking him because we think he had a stroke," he said.

"A stroke?"

I took the elevator up to see my brother. The man next to him was in the worst shape I've ever seen. He was covered with sores from head to toe. He called for his mother and the teddy bear that someone had given him.

"Who's that?" my brother asked each time he called out.

"You!" the guy answered.

Bob and I laughed. What else could we do? The nurses informed me that Bob was slated for tests to see what damage was done to his heart. I accompanied him to every test. When the technicians saw him, they rolled their eyes because they remembered how he carried on each time he had to take an X-ray or MRI.

"Hi, Robert," they said cordially.

"I'm here. Have no fear," I assured them.

The tests were given with no further ado. That night the phone rang at midnight. It's the hospital. *He's dead,* I thought.

"Hello?" I answered cautiously.

"This is Robert Contino. What am I supposed to be doing here?"

"You're supposed to be sleeping. It's midnight."

"I can't sleep. I am opposite the nurses' station and all they do is to cackle, yell, scream, and generally disrespectful of patients' rights. What's really insulting is that their conversations are boring!"

"Calm down. I'll be there tomorrow to cheer you up, okay?"

I did. I am very appreciative that whenever my brother was hospitalized, the nurses permitted me to arrive early and stay after visiting hours to appease him. I am also sure I made their jobs easier.

Days later, Bob was switched to another room, and he was not in a great mood. Every day I brought him the *Sunday* or *The New York Daily News* to keep him occupied as he didn't feel like watching TV.

"You know Bob, when you come home, we should go to a nutritionist," I said.

"I'm not eating fish. I'm not Jewish!" he screamed out for the entire world to hear.

"What are you talking about?" I couldn't get the words out because I was laughing. "I'm not talking about fish. I said a nutritionist!"

"No! No! Your mother's a fag!" he added in a deep threatening voice. "You're Mafia, and Negroes have to work!"

"What the hell is wrong with you? Mommy must be rolling in her grave!"

I started hitting him with the newspaper, screaming myself. Then I stopped because I knew I'd wind up in jail. I was triply mortified as the gentleman in the next bed was black. I didn't know if my brother realized that, as a curtain separated them both. What must he be thinking? I wouldn't mind, but I knew he was one of a few whites who worked in his department, and he liked everyone in his office. I said good-bye and told my brother in a low whisper to shut his damn big mouth. At home, I didn't know whether to laugh or to cry as I was humiliated and didn't want to go back to see him and face the patient in the next bed.

The phone rang at 8 P.M. It was Bob.

"Hi, Sis, whatcha doing?"

"I'm watching television. And you?"

"Nothing. The nurse put the TV on, but I don't want to see anything."

"Are you in a good mood?"

"What are you talking about? I'm always in a good mood. Are you coming tomorrow?"

"Yes," I answered. "Bright and early."

"Okay. Come really early and take me home."

"When we get the test results, all right?"

"Okay," he answered, "good night."

The next day, I put on a big smile and visited my brother. This time he was sitting on a chair, and a Russian aide was cleaning the room. Bob's conversation went as follows:

"Do you know anything about Shakespeare? Did you ever see a Shakespearean play? Have you ever read a Shakespearean play? Do you like Shakespeare?"

She thoroughly ignored him, as I guess she did with most patients, or perhaps she didn't understand English very well. I glanced at the patient in the next bed. He had the blanket rolled up to his chin and look petrified. I smiled a "hello" which he acknowledged with a frozen smile. When he got up to go to the bathroom, I realized that he had a wooden leg. I felt doubly horrible for my brother's behavior. Later, when his family visited him, Bob waved and greeted them cordially.

"You know, he talks for hours," he whispered.

"I'm sure you do, too," I whispered back.

When I inquired about the tests, there were more complaints again from the technicians as Bob had carried on again. Once again, I accompanied him to every testing site. When the hospital cardiologist and technicians saw him, they rolled their eyes because of his outrageous behavior. Now, there was no excuse: the warlord, his sister, sat next to him. I did not leave until every test was done, including a colonoscopy. I threatened Bob with the old man's home saga routine. The comment finally registered as I saw the look in his eyes. He shut up because he knew I meant it this time. I was wearing down from worry. The tests revealed a renal stroke, not a heart attack. I don't know the difference. A stroke is a stroke. He also needed more MRIs because there was some problem in the pancreas area. Once discharged, we rushed to take another MRI for the back of the neck and spinal area that the neurologist requested. We went to the GI doctor to set up the colonoscopy and to have him review the tests Bob took in the hospital. The doctor wasn't too receptive about where the tests were to be taken. I was a little annoyed but thought nothing of it then. Sometime later, I realized that when you call 911, you don't get taken to the Waldorf. You are taken to the nearest hospital to save a life. A week later, he hadn't retrieved the results of Bob's tests. I cancelled the appointment.

I made an appointment to see *Dr. Sand, the GI specialist at the hospital. She was originally the one who suggested my brother having more tests for the pancreatic cancer. I don't know whether someone mentioned the cancer to my brother because Bob was a changed man when he came home, as he rarely smiled. I don't know whether he was in pain because he never confided in me. I do know he lost his appetite or he questioned what I made and why he had to eat it. Usually, we had steak every eight or nine days. One night, he only ate half the steak. The next night, I gave him the other half.

"I thought you said we could only have steak every eight days."

"Bob," I said, "eat the fucking steak."

My friends said he lost his appetite because he was on new medications. I never spent so much time updating the medications sheet that were set up for him, and I faxed or carried the list with us whenever we went to any doctor's office or faxed the changes from doctor to doctor.

I rehired an old friend, Eleanor, who used to take care of my dad and cooked for us. I told her I didn't care what she fed him—just get him to eat. Bob was irritable and I was beside myself, as I, for the first time, didn't see a light at the end of the tunnel. We didn't go out as much because he had a hard time walking. Sometimes he told Charlotte his hip hurt. Bob was entitled to a physical therapist several times a week because he was inactive in the hospital and never left the bed. As usual, he lied and said he could walk, but I paid him no mind; I knew better. Thank God for Ralphie's son, Charles Paturno. Ralphie Paturno was a childhood friend we grew up with. He and his sister, Marie, who was my friend, lived next door to us when we were kids. We're still friends today. Ralphie had passed away years ago. Charles was head of physical therapy at Victory Memorial Hospital at that time (presently has an MBA and is on the staff of Lutheran Medical Center), and was extremely helpful and knowledgeable about patients' rights. Whatever he suggested to help Bob, I did. I requested and received the therapist's service from GHI. As much as Bob liked the therapist, he refused to stand up straight and told me to "shut up" in front of him. I left him with Charlotte and went upstairs to work on my computer.

When we went to Dr. Sand's office, my brother hadn't shaved in nine days and looked disgusting.

"Bubba, bubba, on and on," he sat there saying over and over.

Dr. Sand referred to him as "retarded."

"Retired," I corrected her as sweetly as possible.

She gave us the prescription for the new deciding MRIs as to whether or not he had pancreatic cancer.

"What the hell were you saying in there that she thought you were a retard?" I screamed at him when we left the office.

"Why," he answered calmly, "she wasn't talking to me."

Charlotte calmed me down. She knew he knew he was pushing my buttons, and that I would like to slam him one. Four days later, we showed up at Victory Memorial Hospital for the MRIs. Turned out we were supposed to give the doctor's receptionist the form and get clearance from GHI. Most doctors gave the form to the receptionist themselves and contact us at a later date or do the calls while we wait in their office. The hospital wouldn't let Bob take the tests unless it was cleared. The cashier and I spoke to Dr. Sand who informed me that she was busy and a specialist. I informed her that we weren't leaving until Bob took those tests, stressing that all my brother's doctors were specialists. I was adamant and refused to back down. We were racing against time for these tests. Three hours later, it was a done deal, and we were out of there. Based on these results, I made an appointment with the oncologist for a blood test for pancreatic cancer.

Last Stages

The day Bob died started out as any other day. Charlotte spruced him up for the day. First visitor: the physical therapist. Once he left, off we went to the new neurologist, who informed me that my brother had a problem in the back of his neck, and, unless operated on, would eventually lose control of his arms and legs, and would become wheelchair bound for the rest of his life. That made sense as to why his handwriting had changed over the last year—from neat to indescribable, especially on the health proxy. It also made sense regarding why he didn't like to shave himself. I guess he had this condition for years. He gestured that his hands weren't up to it anymore. I just figured he wanted more services added to his life.

This diagnosis didn't make the day go any better. Bob and I were arguing all day.

"Keep it up and I will drive us off a pier!" I screamed.

"Let me off first, please," Charlotte piped up from the back. Her comment broke the ice and we laughed all the way home.

Later, Marie, our childhood friend, came with us to the oncologist. That evening, Bob was in no better mood than earlier in the day. Usually, Marie was a calming influence on him. This was odd because Bob kept on making us more unsettled because of his visions. He talked more and more about seeing Marie's brother, Ralphie, passing by, or seeing Raffi and Palma. Marie's brother was dead over sixteen years now. Raffi and Palma were, of course, both gone too. I know now that they comforted him because he was calm after they passed him by or he saw them, but I am still not sure why. When he first informed me of these sightings, I was hysterical, but I learned to let it go. Marie just pretended that seeing Ralphie was normal.

Marie escorted him to the doctor's office while I looked for a parking spot. He was also given a blood test, specifically to detect cancer. My brother was in rare form that night, for when the doctor probed his stomach, he carried on so.

"Is he always like that?" asked the doctor.

"I don't know. Today, he's been impossible."

We set up the appointment for Friday and we left.

"You don't understand, I'm sick, I'm sick!" My brother carried on all the way home.

"I'm going to fall," Bob kept saying as we walked upstairs.

"Please," I said, "fall forward or we'll both fall."

We called one of our neighbors who were always anxious to help, who led him to the bed because he couldn't go any further when he reached the top step. He could only lay down there. my brother slid out of the bed again. I called my neighbor again. When he fell a third time, he lay on the floor.

"You don't understand! My stomach hurts," he screamed over and over.

"Would you like me to call 911?" I said as a joke, knowing his aversion to 911.

"Yes! Yes, please do!"

Marie stayed with him as I waited patiently for the ambulance to arrive. I called 911 three times. Usually, they were at the house in minutes. The 911 operator couldn't account for them being so late. Maybe it was because I said, "stomach" and not "heart."

When they showed up, they worked on Bob for over an hour. I ran upstairs to see what was happening. He screamed over and over, "My stomach hurts! My stomach hurts!

"Did he have diarrhea?" asked the EMS driver.

"Yes, we both did. We both had the pneumonia shot. He has congestive heart failure, asthma, emphysema, high cholesterol, and high blood pressure."

"Thank you, Ma'am. Wait downstairs. Let us take care of him."

I went downstairs and let them continue their job.

"It's all over," I looked at Marie.

"Why?"

"He should have been in the ambulance by now."

They came down shortly, carrying Bob out to the ambulance. None of them were smiling; I knew I was right.

"We're taking him to the hospital," said the EMS ambulance driver. "Okay?"

"Sure, no problem. We'll follow."

"It's all over. I know he's gone," I told Marie after they left.

Bob lasted fifteen minutes after arriving at the hospital. We waited for the emergency room doctors to tell us the cause of death.

Bob died of an aneurysm in his stomach. Originally, I thought it was because the doctor had probed his stomach. Later, I understood that the wall was weak and was going to give out sooner or later, no matter what. Marie and I were allowed in to say good-bye. He looked so awful, so old, so in pain; not at all at peace. When I came home, I called the funeral parlor to make funeral arrangements. Then I took out the list for friends and relatives. Some neighbors came in to offer their condolences. We sat down and had many glasses of wine. Marie was in a state of shock. She was talking to Bob for hours, and now he was gone. I was still aggravated that we were arguing constantly and couldn't believe he died so fast on me.

The next morning, the GI specialist called to tell me that they found cancer cells in the blood test taken the night before. She was very apologetic and asked me to call if I needed someone to talk to. I called the oncologist. He was in a state of shock and offered to call any doctor that I needed to call, or if I needed someone to talk to, he was available. What a kind gesture from someone I had only known for an hour!

Planning the wake was a project in itself. I made an appointment to go to the funeral parlor. I called more friends and relatives before I left the house. I also made the most important call for my brother—the office. Bob was retired on paper but never in his heart, for his thoughts were always there. Jason answered first and was truly saddened, as I could tell by his voice. He was redeemed, and I forgave him in my heart for what he said in 2001. Eddie called right after. I gave him all the information he needed regarding funeral arrangements. Once Bob retired, I was glad I was able to drive him and Charlotte a few times a year to the office to see the whole gang. When I called ahead of time to ask if it was all right because I know that sometimes when people retire, the office is less than enthusiastic to see them. Not for Bob!

"Bob Contino? Of course!" they always shouted.

Marie came with me to the funeral parlor. I never gave Bob a retirement party as he was on death's doorstep on 2001. I was going to give him a pre-sixty-fifth-year-old birthday party because I didn't think he'd last that long. The least I could do was to give him the best send-off I could. I told the funeral director that I hoped I wasn't being too fussy, that I had a theater background and wanted everything too look a certain way—simple and not gross. I had Bob clothed in a navy suit as black was too stark and too final. I guess my costume design background kicked in. We selected the proper prayer card and thank-you note. Knowing my brother, I didn't want him to pop up in the coffin if it wasn't the correct card or thank-you note. I hoped the funeral chapel was filled with flowers. It was.

I am not a ghoul, but I hoped that the people would converse as a celebration of a life and not sit there teary-eyed, as people usually do at a wake. I was happy to see people talking instead of looking mournful. Friends and relatives who hadn't seen each other in years shared in my grief, but made it bearable.

Without sounding too gruesome, Bob looked like a young man in his early twenties, a study of peace and serenity—very different from life. No more suffering. I hoped he was at peace and with my parents. But that wasn't up to me now—just the *powers* above. After the funeral at Green Wood Cemetery, we went to his favorite restaurant, La Sorrentina, in Dyker Heights.

The following week, I received a letter from my brother's office. It was a check for $187.85 in lieu of flowers made out to me. Naturally, I cried all day because I knew how much these people in the mailroom make, and I was touched by their generosity. I donated the money in their name to the Danny Thomas Saint Jude Cancer Hospital for Children and asked to have a receipt sent to the office. I sent a letter to the office, thanking them for their generosity.

The day after my brother died, the GI doctor called me to tell me that there were cancer cells present; Bob did have pancreatic cancer. A month later, I went for a physical checkup for myself, and the primary care doctor told me that, possibly, the cancer ate into the artery that caused the aneurysm. I guess it was a blessing in disguise that he died so fast. But, strangely enough, my brother never complained about his stomach before that night. Maybe that was the reason why he lost his appetite. I wondered if the doctors told him that they suspected pancreatic cancer. I told them not to tell him anything. I often wondered if my brother surmised anything.

"So what's with the pancreas? Anything new?" he asked me one day.

"Nothing," I answered. "They checked everything else—so they might as well do the pancreas, too."

Bob never asked any more questions.

Recently, I read that pancreatic cancer is the fastest growing cancer, and there is no way to detect it until it's too late. Sadly, Luciano Pavarotti, that wonderful tenor, passed away from this dreaded disease. Recently, Patrick Swayze and Ben Gazzara, actors, passed from the same disease. As of now, the survival rate is not very high.

Learning from Bob

D ad told me that when my brother was little, the doctors thought he had meningitis. (He didn't; it was just a scare.) Perhaps this was what Dad was referring to, as I never asked him to explain what he meant by that. A few weeks later, Dad saw a program on schizophrenia and turned to me and said, "You know, Bobby's case is very mild. We were very lucky." After Dad died, I saw and read several articles about the causes of schizophrenia that traced it to a childhood virus. Today that definition is listed in Merck's Medical book.

Lucky, I thought? Didn't he see how this illness changed each of us and my brother? It left him without friends, not to mention the permanent guilt that stood in front of my parents all their lives like a banner headline. My mother was convinced that it was her fault because he was hospitalized the day before her birthday. Was this behavior a result of being hospitalized or was it because some were never cured?

Nothing connected to these thoughts until after Dad died.

I have also seen programs on schizophrenia that traced Bob's case to a childhood virus that affects young people when they are between the ages of seventeen to twenty-three. Maybe that was it. Maybe the earlier medications Bob took had an adverse effect. I also read that people with mental problems are heavy smokers. I'm sure the many packs of cigarettes he smoked did not help. It was amazing that he did not have lung cancer.

I know one thing—mental illness does cause those who are the caregivers to change their course or their lives constantly.

"You know, you can't get married," Bob announced one day.

"Why?" I asked.

"You have to take care of me."

"That's ridiculous!"

There is a song from the musical *Gypsy* entitled, "Everyone Has to Have a Gimmick!" I think Bob knew I had to be there for him—that was his gimmick. I know that when people have a hearing loss, sometimes the body compensates, and they have better vision. Perhaps the same is true with mental illness. Without saying anything to me, he managed to have my life revolve around him. It wasn't so ridiculous, as the more I put into caring for my brother, the less time I did have to spend on myself. It got to the point that when I went to the theater at night, I would tell him to stay downstairs and wait for me because I was afraid he would fall down going up to bed. Usually, I called to check in. Bob refused to answer the phone. Of course, I couldn't enjoy myself as I thought he was dead. To top it off, he loved to report me to our senior cousins, Palma and Nettie, now both deceased. When our parents died, Bob and I voted them our surrogate parents and took them out or had them join us for all major holidays. We all got a kick out of that. Bob had an ear to talk to when I came home too late and complained to them.

"She shouldn't be out so late, something could happen to her."

When my cousins told me that, I laughed and said, "Sure, he doesn't want to cook for himself or think. I do all of that for him. He's not stupid."

My brother could come up with other zany ideas to irritate me. He called my cousins to "report me" because there were too many paintings on the walls, and his elbows didn't have too much space as he walked through the house. He "would appreciate it very much" if they could tell me not to buy any more. Huh?

Bob also "reported me" if he thought I spent too much money on any item. Well, some of the times. It depended on the situation and place. When we ate out, which was quite often, he would hand me twenty dollars. Think of what place is only twenty dollars. I referred to him my *Twenty-Dollar Man*. When we ate in Morton's Steak House in New Jersey, he couldn't wait to call our friends and relatives to talk about the most expensive steak he ever had. They must have asked him if he treated me.

"Well, you know my sister. She doesn't care what it costs. It was a treat for me and Charlotte."

However, on the flip side, I limited my time out unless I knew I was coming home before ten o'clock. I gave up having parties because he could be extremely insulting, and I was not in the mood for it. I don't know whether this was a ploy to have me listen to him or because he didn't feel well and didn't want the confusion of dealing with large groups of people. In fact, in the last few weeks of his life, he used the walker in the house and/or a cane again.

"Hey, lady, watch it! Don't you see I have a cane! I'm handicapped!" he yelled when an elderly lady crossed his path.

I was upset because I didn't make the hood to cover my face. Bob was not like that in the past.

Bob loved the good life, good company, good food, and good time. He was known for his sharp sense of humor and knew human nature very well. He could size up a person in one sec. If he didn't feel like talking to someone, he didn't, which aggravated me, to say the least. My other nickname for him was "Mr. Metaphor Man," as he would make comments about people if they didn't shape up to his standards. Most people did not get his humor. He was a very bright guy who was trapped by his own circumstances. He enjoyed being with kids, too, only if he liked the child. When my friend, Suzanne Plavé, adopted a girl named Luisa from China, my brother was taken aback. I think his nose was out of joint as he had to share the spotlight with her. Bob soon got over it and loved when she came over to ask how he was. She made him feel important. When he was sick, she couldn't wait to call him or send him a gift. He loved those moments because it meant more coins in his pocket. From time to time, he spoke to her on the phone before talking to her mother.

A few years back, Bob asked why we hadn't gone to Merilee's home "as usual" on Christmas eves and whatever happened to her, as he always appreciated her time to serve him. (Natch!) I explained that I was insulted because he had not been invited to her daughter's wedding. His eyes welled up with tears, and then he shook his head sadly and said, "Ah, well."

She always made him feel special. I could tell the way his looks thanked her. She, too, appreciated his humor, and he considered her as one terrific lady and a good hostess. And why not? When she served lobster, she asked Bob if he wanted it cracked and taken out of the shell. He said "yes" of course; more service and less chance of getting his hands dirty. Bob could never resist being waited on hand and foot.

Of course, time heals all wounds. God opens a door of one's life as one closes. I took Christmas Eve back to Brooklyn, my hometown. Each year, I invited close friends and relatives to a charming restaurant in Cobble Hill—Marco Polo. We all liked the food and service and piano music because it's festive and Italian—a very traditional Christmas Eve. I rarely spent this holiday in my home since I was a kid. Why? I don't know. I think it's because we were only four people: Mom, Dad, Bob, and me. All my friends had lots of company. We didn't. It was Mom's rule. I guess it was because she came from a large family and wanted a quieter holiday. So be it. My life was now filled with better memories and more responsibilities.

Merilee and her family came to Bob's wake. So, in the end, we came back together. Because after all, we all have family pressures, and sometimes one has to just understand that it boils down to who will be hurt, not whether someone gets hurt. Redemption is merely our recognition that we are all human, and we all need forgiveness, love, and understanding.

I don't understand why Bob was afflicted with so many medical ailments, for as soon as we resolved one, another one surfaced. When I think about now and the time I went through these medical crises with him, I cried a lot but not in front of him, because of the unfairness of it all. I'm grateful to the friends (Marie Pionegro, Suzanne Plavé, her mother and daughter, Alba Savage, Rosalind Panepento, Cathy Goldsmith, Gerri Torres, and my family—the Arenas) who supported me and didn't call me every two minutes. Only one or two did to find out the latest happenings and told the rest. I appreciated that thoughtfulness very much. I am amazed that I had the patience to handle and face my brother's problems with him. I often credit this to the fact that I was a teacher, because when Plan A didn't work, I went to Plan B. We're geared to think in multiple options. I guess I could tap myself on the back for these challenges. I remembered my mother's reaction when I applied to Fordham University, located near City Hall at that time.

"My baby is going to go to Fordham by herself? You don't know how to cross the street by yourself. What do you know about the big city? What if you get hit by a car crossing the street?"

"Mom, what are you talking about? Didn't you live in the big city?" I asked.

"But it was different then and safer."

"Yeah! It was 1917 and now it's 1955. Don't be ridiculous."

I've come a long way now to be a grown-up and a responsible person handling what I have had to do for him today.

In November 2005, Bob would have been sixty-five years old. The city sent me 1,000 dollars in death benefits. He didn't live to be that age, and I never had the opportunity to give him a party for that year. Instead, I hosted a memorial luncheon at La Sorrentina's Restaurant, where we shared Bobby stories. Each year, I did the same. However, when I woke up those days, I thought I am not doing this again, but a little voice said, "Yes, you are." Then, I was never known to do the same thing year after year.

I've always been known as a party person and any excuse will do for a gathering, including a memorial luncheon. Perhaps I do it to come to terms as to why Bobby had so many ailments and me none. I question why horrible people are healthy as horses, and he was a good person and sickly. Maybe it's up to me to educate those who have turned away from friends who are afflicted with the same sickness.

I think about Bob from time to time. A short time ago, I wondered if he was happy or in a sunny place.

My kid cousin, Joanne, called and said, "You have to listen to this. When Phyllis (another cousin) and I were about ten or eleven, we used to stay at Palma's house for a week."

"Sure do remember," I answered. "When you guys were older, I took you to New Hope or Lahaska, Pennsylvania or to other tourist places."

"Well, one time, your brother took us bowling to the park and out to eat."

"You're kidding? I didn't know he bowled. He took you to the park and out to lunch? I'm impressed."

"Yep. I had the strangest dream. I dreamt he picked us up in a big white convertible with the top down. We went bowling to the park and out to eat. We drove over a bridge. I don't know which one it was. Then we drove to your house. The back porch was set up like a solarium, with flowers and water. All enclosed. Beautiful. Absolutely beautiful."

"My God," I said, "I always wanted that, but I realized that anyone could climb from the roof of the garage next door and into my house. Actually, it was a pipe dream. We didn't have the space needed for the solarium. How odd, you should tell me this. I was wondering if Bob was in a warm, sunny, place…if he was happy."

"Oh, it was very warm and sunny that day. Plenty sunny. He wore sunglasses because the sun was so strong. He drove like he didn't have a care in the world. He's happy, very happy."

Recently, my friend Suzanne's daughter, now a high school student, said to her:

"Mom, I miss Uncle Bobby. I saw him, Mom. He looks very happy. He has a young face. His face has no pain. He looks good. He's happy."

Years ago, Bob said to my parents, "What happened to me? I had to have my eyes operated on twice because of a double-cross in my eye. I still had to wear glasses. I went in for tonsils and had my adenoid taken out as well. I had braces on my teeth and got cavities. I had caps put in and they cracked. Even my head wasn't put on straight. What happened to me?"

I don't know, Bob. Maybe we never will, or perhaps the answer is that I am the one who's been chosen to tell the story.

I was amazed at my stamina at spending many hours sitting with my brother in the hospital to keep him calm. Believe me, I sat there many hours writing, writing away either at the doctors' offices or at the hospitals. Was this a way to compensate and get me through the traumas I had to deal with and encouraging him, without saying a word to him? After he died, I read through what I had written, and I was surprised at what I had done on all those snippets of paper. Was this a way for the mind to keep the caregiver focused on the sick person, or am I the chosen one to write about Bob, or better still, that neon sign still shining in front of my eyes from time to time, "What if I wasn't there?"

The following year June, Principal Alan Siegel presented two awards at Bob's alma mater, Lafayette High School for students who overcame diversity. Knowing my brother, he would be happy that he wasn't paying for it and probably figured his sister had nothing better to do.

I recently found his yearbook and saw what he wished for when he graduated: "To be a success in life." I thought, *In life or afterlife?*

Recently, I finished a book, *Born to Create* (Dorrance Publishing Co.) to help others who wanted to be in a creative field and were told by their parents that they had to pick a more lucrative field, i.e., one that pays the rent. Although I spent lots of time caring for my Dad and brother, at least I could say, I still found time to follow my dreams.

And I hope Bob at last has found his.

Bob fishing away without a care in the world